Stretching Man's
Mind: *A History of*
Data Processing

Stretching Man's Mind: *A History of Data Processing*

By

Margaret Harmon

 MASON/CHARTER

NEW YORK 1975

001.609
H225
93481
May 1975

Library of Congress Cataloging in Publication Data

Harmon, Margaret.
   Stretching man's mind: a history of data processing.

   Bibliography: p.
   1. Electronic data processing--History. 2. Computers--History. 3. Calculating-machines--History.
I. Title.
QA76.H2834   001.6'09   74-3403
ISBN 0-88405-282-6

Acknowledgments

To Auerbach Publishers, Inc., for permission to use information in their *Standard EDP Reports* and other publications (cited in the bibliography) without specific citations. This privilege has been exercised in particular in the discussion of data communications, alphanumeric displays, computer output microfilming, and optical character recognition.

To Barnes & Noble Books, Inc. for permission to quote from J. H. Broome, *Pascal.* Copyright 1965. Courtesy Harper & Row, Publishers, Inc.

To Newnes-Butterworths for permission to use numerous diagrams and concepts in Chapter 5 from K. N. Dodd, *Logical Design for Computers and Control.* All rights reserved.

To the International Business Machines Corporation for permission to use Figure 13.1; explanations and illustrations in Chapter 14; and Table 15.1 from *Introduction to System/360*, Manual R29-0256-1, Copyright 1968; and also for the many illustrations credited separately.

To W. W. Norton & Company, Inc. for permission to quote from Ortega y Gasset, *The Idea of Principle in Leibnitz and the Evolution of Deductive Theory.* Copyright 1969.

v

viri memoriae
Arthur R. Harmon

Contents

ix

Introduction

This book is a kind of meandering canoe trip through the country of calculating machines and computers. It is intended for people who are new to this country and want to get a general view of it.

At first the stream down which we paddle is shallow and slow, and we have time to observe the surrounding landscape. Along the way there are many interesting tributaries which join and swell the current of the mainstream, and we examine them as we come to them. Then the current flows faster and faster until it turns into a torrent which changes the riverbed and even the landscape. We have the feeling that we may be rushing toward some precipitous Niagara.

On our journey we will tell about the lives and work of the early inventors because we think these men were interesting people. But as time goes on, the development of the computer becomes less and less personal. Invention itself has now become a science. A new device no longer tends to be the product of one man. It is more likely to be the product of some enterprising company which senses a need for a new type of device and turns loose a whole brigade of researchers and designers to bring it into being.

In this book tributaries to the computer—Boolean algebra, the transistor—have in general been described briefly on the spot as they loom up on the landscape, for those who want such explanations. Our more sophisticated readers may simply skip these little primers. However, we have not described such computer elements as memories and peripherals in the order in which various techniques came into use, but have discussed them by subject. And we have defined the anatomical parts of a modern computer in a glossary. The reader who wants to pursue the subject in more detail is referred to the bibliography.

The reader will note that the designers of the early calculators were different from the members of a modern design team. They were men interested in the whole range of human learning—philosophy, religion, politics, the arts. Modern designers tend to be specialists in mathematics, electronics, or some other narrow field.

José Ortega y Gasset explains this phenomenon. He says of the 16th century:

Philosophy as thinking in terms of necessity was *the* knowledge, was *the* learning. Properly speaking, there was no other, and for its purpose it found itself alone in confronting Reality. Within its ambit the sciences began to be distilled as particular aspects of its "way of thinking." They busied themselves with parts of Being, with particular themes: spatial figures, numbers, stars, organic bodies, and so on, but the way of thinking about these things was philosophic. Hence, Aristotle still calls the sciences *fragments* of knowledge or topics. Modern men of science must swallow, willy-nilly and once for all, the fact that the "strict" character of Euclid's science was merely the quality of "strictness" as cultivated in the Socratic schools, especially in Plato's Academy. Now, all those schools were occupied chiefly with ethics. It is obvious that the Euclidian method, the exemplary "strictness" of the *more geometrico,* originated not in mathematics but in ethics. Whether it would have had better luck in the one than in the other is another question. The sciences, therefore, were born as particular aspects of the philosophic theme, but their method was the same as philosophy's, modified to accord with their fragmentary nature.

Philosophy's position in the modern period, even if considered only in its relation to the sciences, is completely different from the earlier one. During the 16th century and the first two-thirds of the 17th century the mathematical sciences, including astronomy and mathematics, achieved a truly prodigious development. The broadening of their themes was accompanied by a growing refinement of their method, and this in turn was followed by great material discoveries and by really fabulous technical applications. These moved not only with complete independence of philosophy, but actually in conflict with it. The consequence was that philosophy ceased to be *the* knowledge, *the* learning and saw itself only as *one* knowledge, *one* form of learning confronting others. Its theme, given its range and its universality, can still pretend to some primacy, but its way of thinking has not evolved, whereas the mathematical sciences have gone on modifying what philosophy originally taught them, and out of this they have made what are, in part, new ways of thinking. Philosophy, therefore, no longer stands alone confronting Being. There is another court of inquiry, a different one, which is busy searching out the truth of things in its own way; that way is exceedingly precise, superior in certain aspects to the traditional philosophic way. In view of this, philosophy now regards itself as one more science, with a more important theme but a clumsier method.

The development of the computer has received many contributions developed entirely apart from the mainstream and subsequently sucked into it. These include general concepts such as Boolean algebra, general components such as the vacuum tube and the transistor, and working devices such as the teletype, the printer, the camera, and the telephone. Computer designers recognized the so-called technological propinquity of devices like the television tube to the devices they needed, and appropriated them.

Many of these potential contributions to the computer were invented long before they were utilized. The first electronic computer (Atanasoff's) was not designed until about 20 years after the vacuum tube was invented. Eckert says that the computer could have been invented 10 to 20 years earlier than it was. It appears that an invention does not become a reality until there is a combination of adequate technological level, public demand, and money. Babbage could have surmounted the technical difficulties of his calculators if he had had the money and the market for them. There had long been a demand for fast calculators when the ENIAC was invented, satisfied to some degree by the Bush differential analyzer, but money was lacking until World War II came along and the government supplied it. A certain public climate seems also to nurture invention. Perhaps the automobile and the computer have prospered best in the United States because we are less hidebound than older countries and more willing to take a chance on something new and suffer with its growing pains.

What is a computer? According to the general definition of the word, it is anybody or anything that makes computations. (The distinction between comput*or*, a person, and comput*er*, a machine, has become blurred.) Pascal's prototype of the pocket adding machine would therefore be a computer.

But today the word has special technical definitions. The general-purpose digital computer has four essential characteristics:

It manipulates symbols according to given rules.

It does this processing in a predetermined order under the direction of a previously written program.

It has means for taking in the data and the program.

It has the ability to give out the results of its calculations.

There are two general types of computer—digital and analog. In the digital computer, numbers are represented by discrete symbols, and discrete physical states of the machinery form a definite number system. In the analog machine, numbers are represented by continuous quantities such as an electrical potential, or by mechanical quantities such as the rotation of a wheel. The mechanical or electrical quantity is said to be analogous to the actual quantity—hence the computer is called analog. There are also hybrid computers which combine both types. Pascal's calculator is a digital device. It is not a computer because it does not have a stored program.

We talk about *a computer,* but the modern computer is often not a single entity but a collection of units. A computer installation may have one or more central processors, an assortment of card, tape, or disk equipment, printers, microfilmers, graphic plotters, and such scattered around in the same or another room, and also—connected by wire—hundreds of terminals out in the hinterland. These various addenda may be changed at will, so there is really no limit to the variety of possible computer systems.

Modern electronic computers have lived through three generations. The first generation used vacuum tubes; the second used transistors and crystal diodes; the third used silicone chips containing circuit elements so small they can hardly be seen without a magnifying glass.

The fourth generation is still evolving.

chapter 1

The Abacus

We think of a calculating machine as a modern invention, but actually mechanical calculation is thousands of years older than calculation with written numerals. If we include the very earliest counting machine, the fingers, the calculating machine is as old as man himself.

The earliest aids to counting with the fingers were cuts notched in a stick, knots tied in a string, and a handful of pebbles. The shepherd would put down a pebble every time he counted ten sheep on his fingers. The Greeks and Romans used pebbles or disks of glass, bone, or ivory. The Greeks called them *pessoi* and the Romans, *calculi*. It is possible that the shepherd drew lines in the sand and laid down his pebbles according to place value, but the Greeks used a marked counting board or table, the *abakion*, from *abax*, a round platter. The Romans called their counting boards *abaci*.

The word *abacus* was later extended to cover calculating devices on which beads are moved on wires or strings. The Mayans appear to have hit upon this system, using grains of maize threaded in rows of ten. The system of counters on a board was used in Greece at least as early as 500 B.C., and may have been imported from earlier cultures in India, Mesopotamia, or Asia Minor. The abacus of the Greeks and Romans was generally a plain table or board marked with a few parallel lines to show the "places."

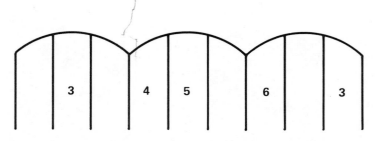

(a) Arc abacus. The number shown here is 30,450,603.

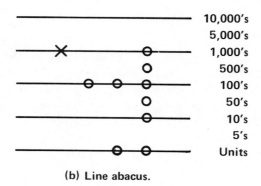

(b) Line abacus.

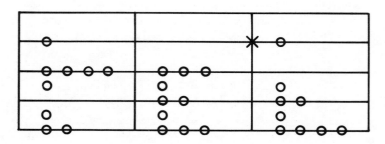

(c) Line abacus. 1457−378=1079.

Fig. 1.1. Abacus.

People often wonder how the Romans ever kept their accounts or calculated the arches of their buildings with the clumsy Roman numerals. Of course they never did. They did their computations on a counting board and merely recorded the results in Roman numerals. People also wonder why the Arabic numerals, with their inestimable advantage of place value, were so slow to be accepted in Europe. The answer is that people already had the advantage of place value in the counting board, and got along very well by doing their sums in two steps—calculation on the board and recording on the tablet.

In the place value system, of course, the position of a number symbol determines its value, and consequently a limited number of symbols can express numbers of any size without the need for repetitions or the creation of new symbols as the numbers get higher. The invention of the place value notation has been called one of the most fertile inventions of humanity, to be compared with the invention of the alphabet, which replaced thousands of picture signs intended to convey a direct representation of the concept in question. Arabic numerals began to penetrate into Europe in the 12th century from the Islamic world, and gradually superseded Roman numerals.

In most number systems throughout history, 5 or some multiple of 5 (10, 20, or 60) has been used as the base—because we have five fingers on a hand. However, there is a number system called Syriac based on 2s and 4s because we have two hands and two feet. In South America, some tribes still give special names to certain groups—one hand for 5, two hands for 10, two hands and one foot for 15, two hands and two feet for 20 (possibly the origin of fourscore).

It is not until we come to the computer than we really stop counting on our fingers. The computer gets away from "hand" calculation in a double sense in that the binary system supersedes the decimal system.

The Greeks used their counters not only on the board, but

also in arrangements of "geometrical numbers"—triangles, right angles, etc. By this means they discovered various laws of number theory—for instance, the rule that the difference between two consecutive square numbers is always an odd number, the "corner."

The Romans had a small hand abacus for simple calculations and a larger counting board with loose counters.

After the decline of Rome, we don't hear much about mathematics and the abacus until we come to Pope Sylvester II, who greatly influenced the study of mathematics. Born Gerbert of Aurillac in Auvergne around 940, he was schooled in a monastery. He made a journey to Barcelona and continued his studies in the Spanish border country. He learned much about mathematics there, and probably also first became acquainted with Arabic numerals, for the Arabs had been in Spain since 713. Gerbert then went to Rheims to study dialectics and teach mathematics, including computations on the abacus. He later went to Ravenna to tutor the emperor's son in arithmetic and then spent some time as adviser to the Pope. Gerbert became a bishop and, in 999, Pope Sylvester II. He died in 1003.

Gerbert wrote *Rules for Computation with Numbers on the Abacus*. His abacus had 72 columns (three for fractions). The columns were sometimes closed off by the "arch of Pythagoras" at the top (Pythagoras was wrongly believed to have invented the abacus). The arch contained the name of the column.

Gerbert's innovation was to use, instead of six pebbles or counters for the number 6, a single counter marked with the number 6. These counters were marked not with Roman numerals, but with nine strange new characters, the Indian or

Arabic numerals, which may have appeared for the first time in Christian Europe on Gerbert's abacus. These counters were called *apices* (perhaps from their form). He had some 1,000 of them carved out of horn.

Gerbert, however, did not understand the system of written numerals already invented by the Arabs; what he did, in fact, was to make the abacus clumsier, because the pieces constantly had to be substituted on the board instead of merely being added to or moved about.

The use of counters in the secular as well as the monastic world may have been due to Gerbert's influence. The counters used for reckoning came to be formalized and of great variety. Brass counters, called *jetons* in French and jettons in English, are believed to have been introduced in England soon after the Norman Conquest. The word comes from the French *jeter*, to throw or cast (hence to cast accounts). Jettons were sometimes called black money. Royal houses had jettons specially made for them, and in the 16th, 17th, and 18th centuries some important families and financial houses copied this practice as a status symbol.

Nuremberg had a small group of manufacturers who appear to have supplied tokens for use in Germany, England, France, and the Low Countries. They were always made of brass, but sometimes resembled current coins and carried a head of the appropriate ruler. These counters often bore a proverb such as *Heut Rot Morgen Todt* (here today, gone tomorrow). Dutch names for counters are *leg-gelt* and *leg-pfennig* (from the act of laying them on a board). The German *rechen-pfenning* means reckoning penny. Many of these counters are still around.

There are, however, very few counting boards or tables to be found. When they were no longer usable for reckoning, they could still be used up as ordinary tables. Counting boards were often mentioned in inventories and wills, and since they were bequeathed to daughters as well as sons, there is evidence that some facility with the counting boards was one qualification for a marriageable daughter as well as an important skill for the educated man of affairs. In 1556, New Year's gifts to the queen, Mary Tudor, included counting tables, counters, and silver boxes for the counters. The King of France would give purses full of counters to important members of his household at New Year's. Sometimes, instead of being marked with lines, the table was covered by a marked cloth. Around 1700 officials would carry these cloths with them to check the calculations made by the local administrators.

Many names and customs from the counting board survive today. The ruled columns in our ledgers probably mirror the arrangement of the boards. The word "bureau" comes from the French *bure*, woolen cloth, which was probably used to cover the counting table; which itself came to be called bureau. By further extension, bureau came to mean the counting room or office, and finally the staff of officials working in it.

The word exchequer, the name for the British royal treasury, goes back to the Old French *eschequier*, a chessboard or counting table, from *eschec*, check (at chess). The Latin word for checkerboard is *scaccarium*, from a Persian word meaning king because the king is the chief piece in chess. Officials of the treasury used to gather around a table covered with the marked exchequer cloth. Part of their duties was to compare the computations on the board with the tally sticks on which sums of money had been recorded; hence the word check for a bank draft.

The exchequer table was used for treasury calculations until about the end of the 18th century. The system of recording the receipt of money by making notches on tally sticks was first introduced to the exchequer by William the Conqueror. The tally system was abolished by Parliament in 1782, but was not finally discontinued until 1826. The tallies were stored in the

Star Chamber, which was packed with them. In 1834, when the room was needed for something else, they were ordered burned. They *were* burned, and both houses of Parliament also burned to the ground in the worst conflagration since the Great Fire of 1666.

An old account describes officials seated around the exchequer table, which was ten feet long by five feet wide. It was bordered by a ledge and covered with a dark russet cloth, divided into squares by intersecting lines, probably marked out with chalk. The column farthest to the right was for pence, the next shillings, the next pounds, and the remaining spaces for scores, hundreds, and thousands of pounds, respectively. About halfway down the table sat the calculator.

References to the counting table abound in literature. In Shakespeare's time Arabic figures had been known in Western Europe for several hundred years, but ordinary people did not understand them. Most people could not read or write and did their reckoning with counters. The clown in *A Winter's Tale* has a problem in sheep shearing, and exclaims, "I cannot do't without counters." And Troilus asks:

> Weigh you the worth and honor of a king,
> So great as our dread father, in a scale
> Of common ounces? will you with counter sum
> The past-proportion of his infinite?

Luther said:

To the counting master all counters are equal, and their worth depends on where he places them. Just so are men equal before God, but they are unequal according to the station in which God has placed them.

The use of Arabic figures became imperative in the 18th and 19th centuries with the development of industry and commerce. Arabic notation was much neater than Roman,

Fig. 1.2. The bead abacus. (*Courtesy of IBM*)

8

Fig. 1.3. The astrolabe. (*Geoffrey Clements*)

especially for writing large numbers, and it had no limits. The industrial revolution made Roman numerals and the counting board obsolete.

The bead abacus is common in Asia. (Figure 1.2.) The Japanese soroban is a sophisticated device which can be used efficiently by experts, but its use requires much study.

Today Arabic pen-reckoning has been superseded by the adding machine, the cash register, and the computer. But some abacus buffs believe that children could most easily gain insight into mathematics by learning to calculate with counters on a board.

As for really early measuring devices, Stonehenge and other such circles are believed to have been constructed to sight positions of the sun and moon and construct a calender from their recurrent positions.

A successor to Stonehenge was the astrolabe, which was used from medieval times to determine the altitude of the sun and other celestial bodies. (See Figure 1.3.) It has been superseded by the sextant. Around 1391 Chaucer put together an unfinished treatise on the astrolabe for the instruction of his son Lewis. One source was a work by the Arabian astonomer Messahala, which Chaucer translated from a Latin copy. Another source was John de Sacrobosco's *de Sphaera*. Here is an excerpt:

Conclusio. To knowe the altitude of the sonne or of othre celestial bodies.
Putte the rynge of thyn Astrelabie upon thy right thombe, and turne thi lifte syde ageyn the light of the sonne; and remewe thy rewle up and doun til that the stremes of the sonne shine through bothe holes of thi rewle. Loke than how many degrees thy rule is areised fro the litel crois upon thin est lyne, and take there the altitude of thi sonne. And in this same wise maist thow knowe by night the altitude of the mone or of brighte sterres.

chapter 2

Early Inventors (Before 1625)

The number of weary clerks who dreamed of a mechanical calculator—or even made a model—is not known, but the invention seems to have been late in arriving, in view of all the accounts kept by commercial clerks and the computations repeated by mathematicians.

The first mechanical calculator that worked is generally conceded to be Pascal's. It could only add and subtract. Leibnitz modified this design to include multiplication and division.

It would be a long and impractical task to describe all the calculators, abortive and workable, that were designed as variations of these early devices. We will describe the most important inventors and inventions in some detail, and note a few others briefly.

Gerbert of Aurillac, Pope Sylvester II (c. 940–1003)

Gerbert is often listed among the inventors of a calculator. His invention (discussed earlier in Chapter 1) was merely a variation on the abacus.

Magnus

The Spaniard Magnus, who lived at about the same time as Gerbert, invented a calculator. It was brass and was shaped like a human head; the figures appeared in its mouth where its teeth should be. How well it worked is not known.

❧ Leonardo da Vinci (1452–1519)

Leonardo da Vinci designed a calculator, but this design, together with a substantial part of all his mechanical designs contained in two manuscripts or codices, was "lost" in the Madrid library for so long that they were only a legend. Apparently they had been numbered incorrectly when the archives were recataloged in the 18th century. Dr. Ladislao Reti, a Leonardo scholar, had been searching among the library's 30,000 manuscripts for the mythical volumes, but the discovery was made accidentally by Dr. Jules Piccus, who was rooting through the library for medieval ballads, or *cancioneros*. Around 1965 he asked for the items bearing missing numbers in the sequence of catalog cards on early ballads. He was supplied with the missing Leonardo manuscripts. He later had the manuscripts authenticated by Dr. Reti.

Leonardo's calculator had 13 decimal wheels and a carry mechanism. Nobody knows whether he ever made a model or whether later inventors knew about his design.

Other devices shown in the lost manuscripts are various chain drives, ball bearings, a device to convert rotary motion into reciprocating motion, and a "bomb" for use against enemy forces. The manuscripts are a systematic treatise on mechanics, and it is not known how many of the devices Leonardo invented himself. However, many scholars believe that, in spite of his great work in painting, sculpture, and music, his greatest work lies in his notebooks. One scholar calls the Madrid discovery one of the great manuscript finds of the 20th century.

Leonardo's ideas for such devices as flying machines were probably forgotten because, as has been said, he "awoke too early in the darkness, while all the others were still asleep." But he did prod a few people awake in biology. He was the first of the modern dissectors—that is, the first to dissect many bodies to learn anatomy, and the first to draw accurate pictures of what he found. He soon saw that Galen's description of the heart, with a passageway between the two ventricles, was wrong, and dared to say that the old authorities were frauds. He wrote:

> I do not understand how to quote from learned authorities, but it is a much greater and more estimable matter to rely on experience. They scorn me who am a discoverer, yet how much more do they deserve censure who have never found out anything, but only recite and blazon forth other people's works. Those who study only old authors and not the works of nature are stepsons, not sons of Nature, who is mother of all good authors.

As an engineer he understood the mechanism and dynamics of the body, and his figures of the muscles, supplemented with philosophical studies of muscular movement, have not been surpassed.

John Napier (1550–1617)

John Napier invented logarithms, and for good measure, also designed a calculating device.

The eighth Laird of Merchiston, Napier studied under the renowned John Rutherford at the University of St. Andrews. Like other scientists of his day, he was caught up in religious controversies and wrote a notable work on the interpretation of the scriptures. As a practical patriot he spent some time inventing instruments of war to repel a possible Spanish invasion—highly reflective mirrors that were designed to use sunlight to ignite ships at a distance, a submarine, and a metal chariot with small holes through which shot could be discharged.

Napier spent his spare time on mathematics, and was burdened by the necessity of "multiplications, divisions, square and cubical expansions of great numbers," which took up a lot of time and were also "subject to many slippery errors." In 1594 he conceived the idea that all numbers could be written in exponential form; 20 years later he published his logarithm tables. The word "logarithm" is from the Greek *logos* (reckoning, reason, ratio) and *arithmos* (number) and means the number of the ratio, or exponent.

If we have a geometrical series (1, 2, 4, 8, 16, 32, 64, etc.) and an arithmetical series (0, 1, 2, 3, 4, 5, 6, 7, etc.) where the base of the geometrical series is 2, any term in the arithmetical series expresses how often 2 has been multipled by itself to produce the corresponding term of the geometrical series. Thus in going from 1 to 32, there have been five steps of multiplications by the ratio 2; that is, the ratio of 32 to 1 is the ratio of 2 to 1 compounded five times. Thus 5 is the logarithm of 32 to a base of 2.

It is apparent that the sum of any two logarithms is the logarithm of the product of the numbers: $9 (= + 6)$ is the logarithm of 512 $(= 2^3 + 2^6)$. In the same way, the difference of any two logarithms is the logarithm of the quotient of the numbers; a multiple of any logarithm is the logarithm of the corresponding number raised to the power of the multiple, and a submultiple of a logarithm is the logarithm of the corresponding root of its number.

Thus when complete tables of logarithms are at hand, addition can take the place of multiplication, subtraction of division, multiplication of raising a number to a power, and division of the extraction of a root of a number. In a sense logarithms serve as a sort of calculator. In the series just given we have chosen 2 as the fundamental ratio or base, but any other number might be chosen. The base of Napier's system is $\ell = 2.71828.$

Napier's tables gave only logarithms of sines, cosines, and

the other functions of angles. In 1615 Henry Briggs of London substituted for Napier's radix the number 10, and before his death succeeded in calculating the logarithms of 30,000 natural numbers to the new radix. Before 1628 the logarithms of all the natural numbers up to 100,000 had been computed. To convert Napierian (also called natural or hyperbolic) into common or Briggs logarithms, it is necessary to multiply by 0.4342944.

Napier's invention of logarithms was comparable to other great inventions in relieving mankind of drudgery. Mathematicians, scientists, and astronomers in particular found their work incomparably easier.

Napier also invented a calculator popularly called Napier's bones. (See Figure 2.1.) The bones were oblong pieces of wood or other material with squared ends. Each of the four faces was divided into squares; the top square carried one of the digits from 0 to 9 and the squares below, the first nine multiples of this digit. The squares other than the top one were divided by a diagonal to accommodate two-digit numbers.

Figure 2.2 shows the rods for the numbers 2, 0, 8, 5 placed side by side, plus another rod without diagonals containing the first nine digits. These rods give the multiples of the number 2085, the digits in each parallelogram being added together. For example, corresponding to the number 6 on the right-hand rod we have 0, 8 + 3, 0 + 4, 2, 1, which gives us 0, 1, 5, 2, 1 as the digits, written backward, of 6 × 2085. Each rod contains on two of its faces multiples of digits which are complementary to those on the other two faces.

The Slide Rule

The slide rule appeared shortly after the appearance of logarithms. In 1620 Edmund Gunther plotted these logarithms on a 2-foot line, known as Gunther's "line of numbers," added

Fig. 2.1. Napier's bones. (*Courtesy of IBM*)

other lines for special work, and placed the group on a 2-foot rule, known as Gunther's scale. Multiplication and division were performed by the addition and subtraction of lengths by means of a pair of dividers.

William Oughtred used two Gunther's lines, in straight and circular form, sliding by each other, in order to do away with the need for dividers. This is the simplest form of slide rule—two rules that can slide on each other until a selected number on one scale coincides with a selected number on the other. The result of the calculation is then read off directly on a third scale. More complicated models have a number of rules. (See Figure 2.3.)

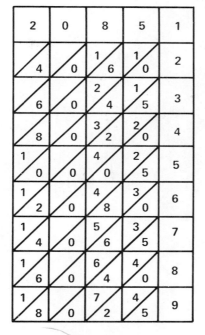

Fig. 2.2.

The slide rule is an analog computer. Numbers are represented by distance on a scale, the distances being determined by the logarithms of the numbers. In general, slide rules solve all problems in multiplication and division, including powers, roots, and proportions.

William Schickardt

In 1623, William Schickardt of Germany wrote to his fellow German, Johann Kepler, describing his first calculating machine, which he said could immediately and automatically add,

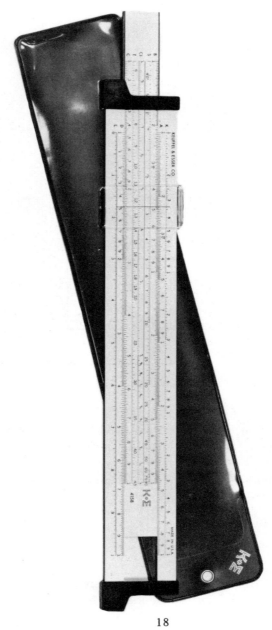

Fig. 2.3. Keuffel & Esser K-12 Prep Slide Rule commonly used for precollege training. (*Courtesy of Keuffel & Esser*)

18

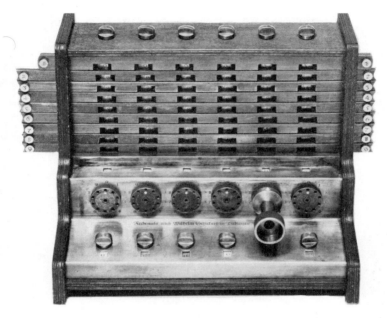

Fig. 2.4. William Schickardt's calculator, designed before 1623. (*Courtesy of IBM*)

subtract, multiply, and divide. It accumulated carries of tens and hundreds by itself, and reversed the process for subtraction. The calculator was destroyed in a fire during the Thirty Years War, but drawings found among Kepler's effects show that the calculator lived up to Schickardt's claims. (See Figure 2.4.)

chapter 3

Blaise Pascal

Blaise Pascal, a many-sided genius, remains a lesser star among the luminaries in mathematics, physics, practical mechanics, philosophy, and literature. We owe to him the early work on modern projective geometry, the first systematic theory of probability, and the theory of the behavior of fluids, from which developed the hydraulic press and—in our day—the science of fluidics. He also gave us the first reliable calculator. His *Provinciales,* a series of letters on religion, are credited with having influenced the reform of the church and having set the style for modern French prose. Perhaps his greatest legacy, however, was the rules for experiment. He taught people how to make scientific investigations—to observe, classify, draw generalizations. He gave us the invention of invention.

Pascal the man interests us as much as Pascal the inventor. We find him appealing and sympathetic in our modern age, perhaps because our age, like his, is one of shifting scientific concepts and shifting values. Broome's account of Pascal's dilemmas strikes a response in us:

The overworked term "crisis" has been applied to various phases in the intellectual history of Europe, including the last years of the seventeenth century, but to none is it more applicable than to the stocktaking period preceding Pascal's birth, when thinkers in France as elsewhere were adjusting themselves to new ideas, and above all to the

21

new *perspectives* revealed by geographical discoveries, by the telescope
and microscope, and the practical or speculative activities of men like
Tycho Brahe, Copernicus or Galileo. ... The upsetting of cosmological
tradition, the reduction of the human scale, the implications with
regard to geocentric theories, and the place of man in the universe—all
these are vital matters for Pascal, and matters on which, moreover, it
would be unreasonable to expect a settled attitude. ... As a man, it may
be said that he reveals almost equally in his life the predictable
reactions of curiosity and anxiety; but the corollary to this is that as a
thinker he is increasingly concerned to find a moral perspective in
which it may be possible, if not to triumph completely over this tension,
at least to understand, accept and live with it....

Much of his mature thought is directed to moral problems, and
the answering of the practical questions: *what must I do?* or: *how should
I live?*

Pascal was born in 1623 in Clermont. His father, Etienne,
was a lawyer and mathematician. He had two sisters, Gilberte
and Jacqueline. Their mother died in 1626. Five years later their
father gave up his job to tutor his children and moved the family
to Paris. Etienne Pascal had advanced theories of education: he
believed in encouraging the natural curiosity of a child and in
not pushing him so hard that his confidence was destroyed. He
did not have to push Blaise in mathematics, for the precocious
child discovered geometry all by himself. His father was so
impressed that he gave him a copy of Euclid.

Blaise never went to school. His stimulus came from his
father's friends, many associated with Father Mersenne's academy, an early center of scientific study. Here Blaise met
Roberval, Desargues, Fermat, and Descartes. Desargues interested Blaise in the study of conic sections, which had intrigued
Plato, Omar Khayyam, Kepler, and many others. Pascal said his
own work was based on that of Apollonius. (See Figure 3.1.)

Desargues went beyond the geometry of his time and
formulated the essential theory of perspective, the basis of
projective geometry. Pascal accepted and developed Desargues'

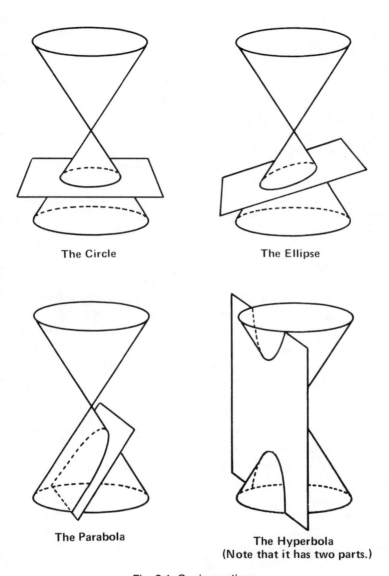

The Circle

The Ellipse

The Parabola

The Hyperbola
(Note that it has two parts.)

Fig. 3.1. Conic sections.

ideas. Before he was 16, he wrote a work on conic sections which Descartes insisted couldn't have been written by one so young.

About this time Pascal formulated what is known as Pascal's Theorem: If a hexagon be inscribed in a conic section, the intersections of opposite sides are three points in a line. Pascal called this his mystic hexagram. (See Figure 3.2.)

In Paris the family moved in high social as well as academic circles, and Jacqueline was presented at court to Anne of Austria. In 1638, however, Etienne helped to organize a protest against a policy of the treasury. When Richelieu found out about it, Etienne was threatened with the Bastille and had to hide out in Auvergne. He was pardoned after Jacqueline made a dramatic appeal to the cardinal, and was made a special tax commissioner in Normandy.

The job was difficult. A public rebellion against the heavy taxation to pay for the war against Austria was put down without settling the fiscal problems Etienne had been sent to handle. Blaise was soon drafted to help his father with the tax business. Pascal was interested in abstract mathematics but had no love for the drudgery of calculating taxes. He conceived the idea of inventing a mechanical calculator; he knew of Napier's work, and possibly also of Schickardt's.

Aside from Schickardt, however, whose device never reached the market, Pascal gets the credit for inventing the first mechanical digital calculator able to do addition and subtraction. In 1642 he engaged a mechanic in Rouen to help him and in two years produced the first model of what he called *la Pascaline.*

La Pascaline seems simple to us since we are familiar with its principle in every pocket adding machine and speedometer. (See Figure 3.3.) The device consisted of toothed wheels with parallel horizontal shafts. All the wheels were decimal except two, which had 20 and 12 divisions, respectively, for *sous* and *deniers*. Each decimal wheel of course had 10 teeth. A carry

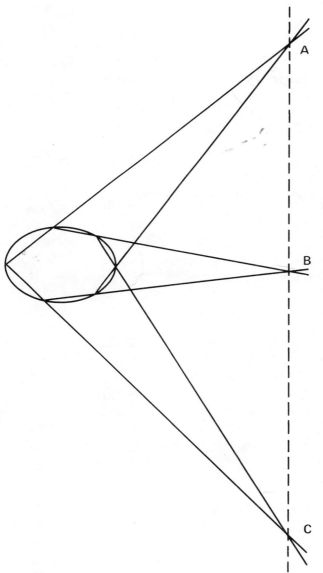

Fig. 3.2. Pascal's Theorem. A, B, and C are the points of intersection of the opposite sides of the hexagon inscribed in the ellipse, and these points are collinear (in the same straight line).

25

ratchet coupled each wheel to the next higher one; as the first wheel completed a revolution, it moved the second wheel a part of the revolution (one-tenth, if the second wheel was decimal). The positions of the wheels could be seen and numbers could be read through windows in the cover. Numbers were entered via dials with slots in which the operator inserted a pointer.

The calculator could add a column of eight figures. A three-digit number would be entered on three wheels and would appear in the window. When a number to be added was entered in the same way, the window showed the total. A metal bar could be moved to show the remainder in subtraction in a second set of windows.

Multiplication was done by a series of additions. To multiply 249 by 54, the operator entered 249 four times, beginning with the right-hand digit. He then entered 249 five times, beginning with the next or tens dial. The total then appeared in the window. Division was done in reverse, by subtraction.

Some ten models of *la Pascaline* are still in existence.

Pascal pointed out that his calculator was a third and entirely new method of calculation. It was faster and more reliable than the old methods of counters on a board or pen-reckoning. The old methods required thought, either in laying out the counters or in calculating in the mind the figures to write with the pen. The inventor of *la Pascaline* had done this thinking beforehand, and the results were automatically supplied to the user.

For many years Pascal kept improving his calculator, and made more than 50 models, trying to make his calculator handle fractions and square roots. His knowledge of projective geometry helped him visualize and lay out the wheels and gears. Each gear tooth had to be filed to size and hand fitted into the gear wheel. The carry ratchet was a new invention.

La Pascaline electrified the world of science. Up to that

Fig. 3.3. Pascal's *Pascaline*. It was 14x5x3 ½ inches. (*Courtesy of IBM*)

time many wonderful devices had been designed, such as Leonardo's flying machine and Napier's submarine, but few had been built. Pascal had actually produced a working model. Thomas Hobbes hailed it: "Brass and iron have been invested with the function of brain, and instructed to perform some of the most difficult operations of mind."

Pascal sent models of *la Pascaline* to influential friends and demonstrated it in the salon of Richelieu's niece. But nobody bought it. It seemed to be too complicated and might be the devil to repair if it broke down. Although it could do as much work as a half-dozen men, it might cost as much as their wages—and the men thrown out of work might make trouble.

Blaise at least enjoyed the wide reputation his invention brought him, and became more and more involved with both religion and science—not a paradox in his day. Scientific and religious thought intersected at many points. One point was the problem of infinite quantities, which seemed to him incomprehensible, and therefore an argument for the limitations of the intellect and the necessity for religion. Pascal now turned to a study of the Jansenist doctrines, named for the theologian Cornelius Jansen or Jansenius (1585–1638). The Pascal household was converted to Jansenism.

This was Pascal's so-called first conversion. It did not lessen his interest in science. In 1646 he began the first of his important experiments.

The Italian Torricelli had recently experimented with a tube of mercury turned upside down in a vessel containing mercury. The mercury in the tube dropped only part way down the tube, and scientists debated whether the space left in the tube was in fact a vacuum, such as nature was supposed to abhor. Some thought it was and others thought that air was somehow seeping in through the pores of the tube. Still others believed that some other mysterious substance was present, since a vessel filled with nothing must surely collapse.

Etienne, Blaise, and a friend repeated the experiment. The water level in the tube fell to about 32 feet. It was plain that 32 feet was the limit of nature's abhorrence of a vacuum above water. After many experiments Pascal concluded that this level had nothing to do with any resistance to a vacuum, but was caused by an external force, atmospheric pressure. His *Great Experiment Concerning the Equilibrium of Fluids* was published in 1663.

An excerpt from this work follows.

CHAPTER 2. *Why liquids weigh in proportion to their height*

It is seen from all these examples that a mere thread of water can counterbalance a great weight; it remains to show the cause of this multiplication of force; that is what we shall do in the following experiment.

If a vessel full of water, closed on all sides, has two openings, one a hundred times larger than the other, with a piston carefully fitted to each, a man pressing the small piston will match the strength of a hundred men pressing the piston in the hundredfold greater opening, and will overmaster ninety-nine.

And whatever be the ratio of the openings, if the forces applied to the pistons are as the openings, there will be equilibrium. Whence it is apparent that a vessel full of water is a new mechanical principle and a new machine for multiplying forces to any amount desired, since a man by this means will be able to lift any burden proposed.

And we must find it wonderful to meet again in this new machine that fixed order which is found in all the old machines, such as the lever, the wheel, the endless screw, etc., which is that the distance covered is increased in the same ratio as the force.

Pascal's principle, now a part of every schoolboy's mental furniture, is:

Pressure is transmitted equally in all directions throughout a mass of fluid at rest, or if the pressure at any point is increased, it is increased everywhere throughout the fluid mass by the same amount.

After his father died in 1651 and his sister Jacqueline entered the Jansenist community in 1652, Blaise eased his loneliness by making a number of friends. One of these, the Chevalier de Méré, interested Pascal in the mathematics of probability by asking: (1) What is the minimum number of throws of two dice necessary to make it worthwhile to gamble on two sixes turning up? (2) How should the stake money be fairly divided among gamblers who stop their game before the normal finish? In working out the answer, Pascal had the beginning of a progression, and saw the possibility of a general method that could be used in much more complicated problems. He developed what is called Pascal's triangle, although it seems the idea had been hit upon previously in Europe and China. The triangle can be extended indefinitely on the pattern shown in Figure 3.4. Each number is the sum of the two immediately above it. The triangle may be applied to some simple forms of gambling, such as throwing coins, to give all the probabilities. For example, the numbers in the fifth row add up to 16, which is the number of different ways in which four coins tossed together can fall. If the numbers in the row are put over 16 (1/16, 4/16, etc.), we have the probabilities of the 16 possibilities in the fall of four coins.

Pascal's *Treatise on the Arithmetical Triangle* is the foun-

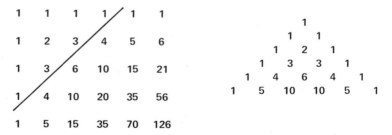

Fig. 3.4. Pascal's Triangle.

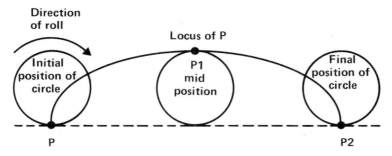

Fig. 3.5. The Cycloid. This curve is the locus of a point on the circumference of a circle which rolls, without sliding, along a fixed straight line. It is shown for one revolution.

dation of modern statistical methods of handling problems ranging from biology to insurance.

After he was 30, Pascal turned more and more to religion, and achieved a mystical experience known as his second conversion. He lent his pen to the defense of the Jansenists. In 1658, however, he interested himself in the problems of the curve known as the cycloid, a popular subject with Roberval and other mathematicians of the time. (See Figure 3.5.)

Soon after that he became an invalid, and spent what energy he had in helping the poor and cutting loose his ties with the world and even with his own family. He wrote, "It is unjust that anyone should attach himself to me ... for I am not an end and aim of anyone."

In his last months Pascal continued his good works, rescuing a young beggar girl and taking a family of paupers into his own house. He died in 1662, at the age of 39.

chapter 4

Successors to Pascal

Sir Samuel Morland (1625–1695)

Morland combined his work as inventor with another career, that of statesman. He was secretary to Oliver Cromwell and later Master of Mechanics to His Majesty King Charles II.

Morland designed three different types of calculators. In 1663 he built a trigonometrical calculating machine, and in 1666 a calculator that seems to have been much like Pascal's. He also described another machine adapted for multiplication and division; its basic principle was the same as Napier's rods but disks were used instead of the rods. A steel pin moved a series of dial plates and indices. (See Figures 4.1 and 4.2.)

Morland's designs represent a distinct advance in the art. However, his machines had the same drawbacks as Pascal's —they were expensive, since they had to be made by hand, and people were leery of the problems of repair. They were not a commercial success.

Gottfried Wilhelm Leibnitz (1646–1716)

Like Pascal and Napier, Leibnitz was an inventor/mathematician. However, he seems to have confined his efforts at

33

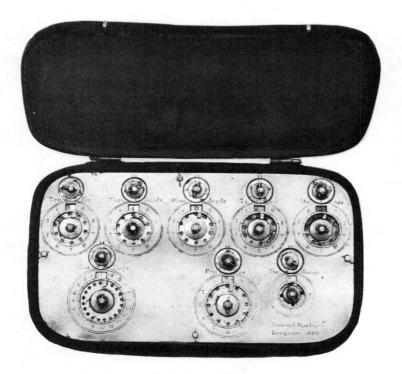

Fig. 4.1. Morland's adding machine. (*Courtesy of IBM*)

machine design to his calculator. The rest of his great body of original work was in theoretical subjects—mathematics and philosophy.

Leibnitz was born in Leipzig about the time Pascal perfected his calculator. His father, a professor, died when Gottfried was six. The boy was largely self-educated, and was quite equal to the task: he was fluent in Latin and knew some Greek when he was 12, and then began the study of logic. At 15 he began the study of law at the University of Leipzig. His dissertation was a famous paper, "De principio individui."

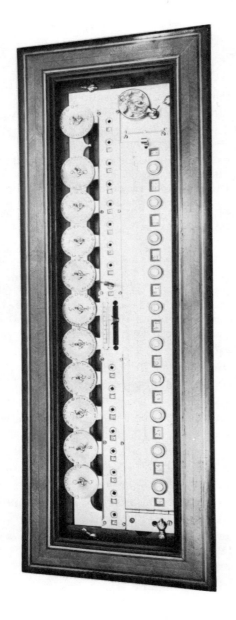

Fig. 4.2. Morland's multiplying machine. (*Courtesy of IBM*)

Leibnitz had a taste of politics in a job with the Elector of
Mainz, and was to spend long years as librarian to the Duke of
Brunswick at Hanover. His real vocation, however, was as a
developer of abstract systems of thought. He was a genius at
organization and synthesis. José Ortega y Gasset says:

The person of Leibnitz coincides with a new impulse toward integration
in European life.... It was then that Europe came—I will not say nearest
to but certainly the least far from—achieving a reunion of the Christian
professions of faith. To this undertaking Leibnitz, as is well known,
dedicated a great part of his effort and enthusiasm....

The movement of integration does not spring from the psychology of
Leibnitz, but vice versa; Leibnitz is an integrator because the whole
history of Europe, having reached the culmination of its progress,
determined that magnificient project and made it possible. Of himself,
Leibnitz put into it the capacity to raise it to a peak with his exceptional
gifts and the circumstances of his education which allowed him to
absorb almost all the principal disciplines when still an adolescent.

When Leibnitz first studied logic, he found himself "greatly
excited by the division and order of thoughts which I perceived
therein." He envisioned a "muster-roll of all the things in the
world," and dreamed of a universal language in which all
nations could communicate. He transformed this idea into a
universal language of concepts after he had become fascinated
by the theories of Ramon Lull. Leibnitz tried to formalize Lull's
system. In his 1666 *Dissertation de Arte Combinatoria* he listed
possible combinations of premises and conclusions and also the
number of valid syllogisms. Leibnitz's discoveries about the
calculus are believed to be connected with his study of symbols
for this work.

Leibnitz built his calculator in 1671 after a study of the
devices of Pascal and Morland. He improved on these machines; his calculator could not only add and subtract, but could
also laboriously multiply and divide. (See Figure 4.3.) In 1673 he

Fig. 4.3. The Leibnitz calculator. (*Courtesy of IBM*)

exhibited his calculator in London, and was made a member of the Royal Society, largely on the strength of his new invention.

Leibnitz and Newton both laid claim to inventing the calculus. Ortega says: "Leibnitz lived in perpetual conflict with Newton. This polemic became one of the most awe-inspiring battles between giants that has ever occurred on this planet."

The calculus deals, among other things, with the rate of change of quantities that vary. For example, if we change the radius of a circle, we also change its area, and we say that the area of a circle is a function of its radius. The ratio of these rates of change is called the differential coefficient, and the means by which the ratio is worked out is called differentiation. If we want to work in the opposite direction, that is, to calculate the variable quantities from a knowledge of their rates of change, the process is called integration. This process can handle many other problems, including the calculation of involved areas and volumes. The differential and integral calculus together are known as the infinitesimal calculus.

Leibnitz introduced the symbol d (for differentiation) instead of the dot used by Newton. He also introduced the summation sign of an elongated s.

Leibnitz's contributions to science and philosophy are too numerous to explain in detail. His philosophy ruled the schools of Germany for nearly a century, and largely determined the developments that superseded it. His theory of monads, the tiny particles that are the building-blocks of both matter and mind, foreshadowed the modern molecular theory and the theory of the unconscious.

Of Leibnitz, José Ortega y Gasset says:

His philosophy is . . . not *oriented* in physics. It could not be, because he himself, together with Newton, is one of the creators of physics. He belongs to the same generation as Newton (1642–1727). The exceeding richness of his thought makes us uneasy even today, as though we were in the presence of an extra-human hyperlucidity, of an ever-phosphorescent soul, which, creating entire sciences while traveling in a stagecoach, kept him from ever giving systematic expression to his hypersystematic ideas....

It has been said many times, and not without reason, that if Aristotle's was the intellect having the most universal capacity in the ancient world, so was the mind of Leibnitz in the modern world. Of the basic disciplines of the "intellectual sphere" there is none which Leibnitz did not possess and, what is more surprising, none on which he did not leave a creative imprint. He renews logic in a most original form, he broadens the domain of mathematics in a fabulous manner, he reforms the principles of physics, fertilizes biology with new hypotheses, purifies juridical theory, modernizes historical studies and gives linguistics new horizons by proposing the great theme of comparative grammar. On top of all this, he constructs a philosophic doctrine which in its details is one of the most complete and most beautiful that has ever existed.... It must be noted that it is *Leibnitz, of all of the past philosophers, from whom came the greatest number of theories current today*. Today is, of course, not tomorrow.

Voltaire amused himself by ridiculing Leibnitz for one of his doctrines—namely, that this is the best of all possible worlds. But Ortega sets us straight on this problem. Leibnitz did not believe that a perfect world was possible—a world free from error, misery, and evil. He only asserts that this is the best world possible under the circumstances. Ortega says:

Leibnitz, for all his famous optimism, does not affirm that the world is good *simpliciter*, but only that it is the best of the possibles, which means that the rest are less good, therefore that they include greater evil, therefore that they are worse. Here is how, on affirming that our world is the best possible, he recognizes only that—strictly speaking—it is the best of those that are not good, therefore of the bad .... All this is an example of the peculiar euphemistic style of Leibnitz because, stated in his own precise terms, it means that *actually* optimism is irrational.

In 1714 George of Hanover was made King of England. Apparently he disliked Leibnitz, and when the Court moved to

London, Leibnitz was not allowed to go along, but was left
behind in his library. The clergy disliked him too because they
thought he was an atheist, but he kept on working and writing in
spite of all this hostility.

He died in 1716, and not one member of the Court of
Hanover followed his body to the grave. A witness said that he
was buried "more like a robber than what he really was, the
ornament of his country."

Grillet de Roven

Another man who dreamt of turning over the drudgery of
arithmetic to machines was a Frenchman, Grillet de Roven. He
built a mechanical calculator in 1678 which had a carrying
mechanism.

Giovanni Poleni

This Italian marquis built a calculating machine in 1709.
He explained that he could give instructions to the device by
setting various levers and the machine would then automatically
go through the prescribed sequence. Poleni was thus an innovator in programming calculating devices.

Charles Stanhope

Viscount Mahon, afterward Earl Stanhope, was another
part-time scientist; his other career was politics. He sympathized
with the French Revolution, disapproved of the war with the
American colonies, and took up the cause of the slaves. He
married Lady Hester Pitt, sister of William Pitt. However, when
Pitt went back on the liberal principles of his early days,
Stanhope opposed the policies of his ministry.

Stanhope was a fellow of the Royal Society when he was 20. In addition to his work on calculators, he experimented with canal locks and steam navigation, and invented a printing press and the microscopic lens named for him. His *Principles of Electricity* was published in 1779.

Stanhope invented three different calculating machines, which were made in 1775, 1777, and 1790, respectively. The first was a multiplying machine in which the Leibnitz stepped-reckoner device was used. The second used a cam plate to bring a variable number of teeth into action. The last was an improvement of Morland's adding machine. The Stanhope demonstrator was a machine for working problems in inductive logic. (See Figure 4.4.) Babbage used Stanhope's devices as a foundation for his own calculator.

The most famous of Stanhope's six children was Lady Hester Lucy Stanhope (1776–1839). In 1803 she became secretary to her uncle, William Pitt. After his death she found she had acquired a taste for active life and went to the Levant and settled among the Druses, a sect which practiced a hybrid religion, part Moslem and part Christian. Lady Hester adopted the religion and settled in a convent, from which she administered the district.

Logic Machines

Various men tried their hands at solving problems in logic by mechanical means, and we will list them here. We have already briefly mentioned Lull and Stanhope.

Ramon Lull, who influenced Leibnitz so profoundly, was a Spanish monk of the 13th century. He constructed what he called his divine wheels, with which he said he could solve all sorts of problems by means of logic.

Lord Stanhope's Demonstrator was a crude machine for working problems in inductive logic.

William Stanley Jevons (1835–1882) also attempted to solve

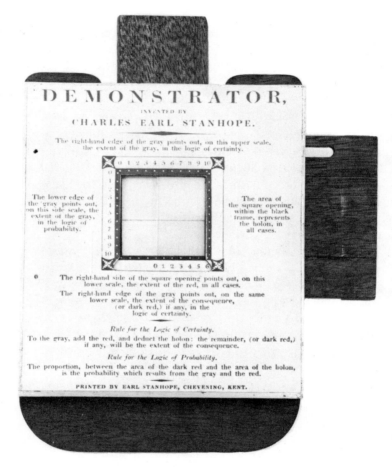

Fig. 4.4. The Stanhope Demonstrator. (*Courtesy of IBM*)

logical problems by a mechanical device. He was an economist
and logician, and in 1864 he published *Pure Logic: or, the Logic
of Quality apart from Quantity*. It was based on Boole's system of
logic, but discarded Boole's mathematical system. Jevons then
spent a lot of time in the construction of a logical machine for

obtaining by mechanical means the conclusion that could be derived from any given set of premises. (See Figure 4.5.) It was shown before the Royal Society in 1870.

In 1881 an American, Allan Marquand, built a machine to handle problems in propositional logic.

Charles L. Dodgson, a mathematician and logician (who wrote *Alice in Wonderland* under the pen name Lewis Carroll) devised a logic machine in 1886. It was a kind of logic abacus and consisted of a ruled board and small counters to be properly placed to solve problems in mathematics and logic.

Charles Xavier Thomas

The first successful calculating machine manufactured on a commercial scale was the arithmometer, invented by Thomas in 1820. It has a driving wheel with nine rows of teeth side by side, the rows having from one to nine teeth each. A movable recording wheel is engaged with one of these rows, and is advanced according to the number of teeth in the row. It is sometimes called the Colmar machine from its place of manufacture in France. The arithmometer is complicated and hard to maintain, but Payen of Paris manufactured an improved version in quantity, and some units are still in service in France.

Baron Wolfgang von Kempelen's Turk

Can machines think? This problem has occupied Alan Turing and many others. But there was one machine that could think because it had a human brain inside it. This machine, the Turk, was one of the famous hoaxes of history.

The Turk was a chess-playing robot who was born in Vienna in 1770 in the brain of Baron Wolfgang von Kempelen, a hydraulics engineer. It was a life-sized wooden figure, turbaned and robed, seated in front of a wooden chest six by two by three

Fig. 4.5. The logical piano of William S. Jevons. (*Geoffrey Clements*)

feet in which a man was hidden so that he could not be seen even when doors were opened and a candle held up to illuminate the inside of the chest.

The Turk always played white, and the chess pieces were magnetized so that they attracted metal disks beneath the board. The man could thus follow the moves and duplicate them on a little peg set inside. He started the Turk by turning a concealed crank. A great grinding and groaning then ensued, and the Turk's left arm (he was left-handed) would hover over a piece and pick it up with mechanical fingers. He would indicate an illegal move by beating his breast, and would wag his head for other signals.

The robot bamboozled and entertained all classes of people for 40 years on the continent of Europe. He met and played Frederick the Great, the Grand Duke of Russia, and Napoleon. He then moved to London and repeated his success. He came to America in 1826, where he was promoted by John Maelzel and William Schlumberger. Maelzel bought the Turk after von Kempelen's death. Schlumberger, the man in the box at the time, was a fine chess player and a ventriloquist, and announced his moves in French. The Turk ultimately made his home in Philadelphia.

Edgar Allan Poe was one of those who suspected the Turk's secret, but it was not made public until 1837, by a disgruntled former employee of Maelzel's. In 1840 the Turk was put into the Chinese Museum in Philadelphia. When the museum burned 14 years later, no newspaper mentioned the Turk's demise.

chapter 5

George Boole and Boolean Algebra

One of the essential contributors to computer development was George Boole (1815–1864), an English logician, mathematician, and teacher. Boole was one of the innovators and the principal developer in his time of the algebra of logic, which expresses and manipulates problems in logic by mathematical symbols. In 1854 he published *An Investigation of the Laws of Thought, on which are founded the Mathematical Theories of Logic and Probabilities.*

Boole did not regard logic as a branch of mathematics, but merely used mathematical symbols and methods. He demonstrated, however, that logic is mathematics restricted to the two quantities 0 and 1. Boole used letters, such as x, y, and z, to represent common adjectives and nouns. He used 1, or unity, to stand for the whole world of all conceivable objects. If, for example, x is taken to represent tigers, $1 - x$ stands for everything in the world that is not a tiger. If y represents lions, then $(1 - x)(1 - y)$ stands for everything that is neither a lion nor a tiger. Boole showed that symbols like these obey certain laws of combination and can be added, subtracted, and multiplied.

Boole also presented a general system of logical inference for propositions having any number of terms. By treating the premises symbolically, he was able to draw any conclusion logically contained in the premises. He also tried to reduce probabilities to the same kind of system, so that if the probabilities of any series of events were known, the probability of any other logically related event could be determined.

But what has all this to do with computers? Well, a computer is supposed to simulate our processes of thought when we add, subtract, and do other calculations, and before we can make a machine that will think, we must analyze our own thought processes. Logic is the study of the rules of thought. We formulate our thoughts in words after we learn to talk, and grammar is a clue to logic. What Boole did was to make it possible to handle the statements of language by means of symbols, in a kind of shorthand. We can see how enormously useful such a system would be when we try to transfer the rules of thought to the computer.

In logic the individual members of a class are called elements. A chair may belong to the different classes of chairs, furniture, and plastic objects. Some classes include or overlap others. The class of furniture includes the class of chairs. The classes of chairs and wooden objects may have common elements, but neither includes the other. The classes of cats and dogs do not overlap at all.

In a statement we say something that may have meaning or may be nonsense. In logic a statement with meaning is called a proposition. It may be true or false, and its truth or falsity is called its truth value. We can express logical relations (includes, does not include, overlaps, is true) by words. Boolean algebra expresses these relationships by symbols.

Boole's new system remained more or less an intellectual curiosity until the 20th century. In his master's thesis (MIT 1938), Claude Shannon showed how Boolean algebra could be used in the design and simplification of complex circuits such as are used in electrical relay circuits and electronic computers. One hypothesis is that we think with our nervous system and record a thought by changes in the electrical or chemical state of nerve elements. The computer "thinks" with circuits, and records a fact by changes in the circuit's electrical state. The combinations of these circuits can be represented by Boolean algebra. We have said that logic is mathematics restricted to the two quantities 0 and 1. Values in a computer circuit are also restricted to these two quantities.

The first calculators, such as Pascal's, used the familiar decimal system, sometimes modified to count money. It worked for mechanical calculating machines, which operate with teeth on gears because there is no problem about cutting ten teeth on a gear. However, when electronic computing devices began to appear, the decimal system lost its popularity. Although theoretically you can have ten—or an infinite number—of different levels of output on a vacuum tube, it isn't easy in practice to hold these levels constant because the plate current on the tube weakens as the tube ages. The levels of current aren't fixed and positive like the teeth on a gear.

The only thing you can count on a vacuum tube or a transistor to tell you is whether it is OFF or ON. Finally the idea surfaced that such a device should therefore count by the *binary* system, which is based on the number 2 instead of the number 10. (The binary system is explained in Chapter 14.)

We can briefly study Shannon's "switching logic," and confine ourselves to the logic of the circuit, not the electronics. The logic holds good whether the circuits use tubes, transistors, magnetic cores, thin films, or other components found in computer circuits.

We will represent switches in Figure 5.1 as *a*, *b*, and *c*. In a series circuit, current will flow only when all switches are closed. In a parallel circuit, current will flow if any one switch (or more than one) is closed.

We can represent the conditions for current flow in Figure 5.1(f) on a chart:

A	B	CURRENT
open	open	no flow
open	closed	no flow
closed	open	no flow
closed	closed	flow

We can use symbols instead of words to describe this circuit, as follows:

0 represents an open switch, or no current flow
1 represents a closed switch, or current flow
• represents the logical AND operation; that is, A • B is read as A and B.
(Note that the dot does not mean the same in Boolean algebra as it does in regular algebra, where the dot of course means multiplication.)

Now we can substitute these symbols in the chart we have just made:

A	B	A • B
0	0	0
0	1	0
1	0	0
1	1	1

And from this chart we can make a table for a series circuit:

$$0 \cdot 0 = 0$$
$$0 \cdot 1 = 0$$
$$1 \cdot 0 = 0$$
$$1 \cdot 1 = 1$$

And now we can make a rule:

$A \cdot B = 1$ only when $A = 1$ and $B = 1$
$A \cdot B = 0$ otherwise

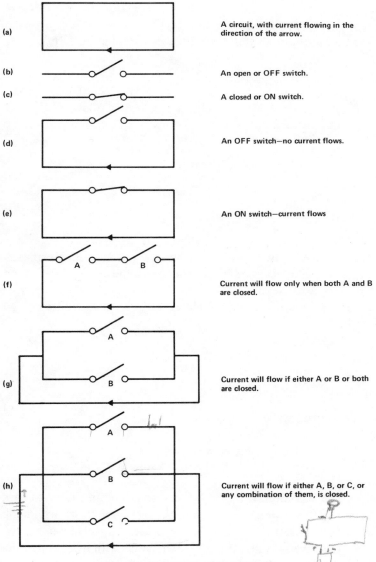

(a)   A circuit, with current flowing in the direction of the arrow.

(b)   An open or OFF switch.

(c)   A closed or ON switch.

(d)   An OFF switch—no current flows.

(e)   An ON switch—current flows

(f)   Current will flow only when both A and B are closed.

(g)   Current will flow if either A or B or both are closed.

(h)   Current will flow if either A, B, or C, or any combination of them, is closed.

Fig. 5.1. The logic of the circuit.

51

We can go through this same process with Figure 5.1(g):

A	B	CURRENT
open	open	no flow
open	closed	flow
closed	open	flow
closed	closed	flow

A	B	A + B
0	0	0
0	1	1
1	0	1
1	1	1

Here + means the logical OR operation, and A + B is read as A or B (+, like the dot, does not mean the same thing as in ordinary arithmetic).

Our table for a parallel circuit comes out as follows:

$$0 + 0 = 0$$
$$0 + 1 = 1$$
$$1 + 0 = 1$$
$$1 + 1 = 1$$

And we can make another rule:

A + B = 1 if A is 1, B is 1, or both are 1.
A + B = 0 only if both A and B are 0.

The equation $1 + 1 = 1$ takes some getting used to, but remember that we are here using the old symbols of arithmetic to represent logical relationships and to form logic equations.

We have said that the computer thinks with its circuits. The basic functions of the arithmetic and control units of a computer are to duplicate some of our simple processes of thought. These simple elements of "thought" in a computer are called logic elements.

One basic logic circuit in a computer is often called a gate. (Storage [bistable] elements are also basic to counting and storing.) Such a circuit has an output dependent on some function of its input. Some such circuits have an output when any or all of a designated set of inputs are received within a specified time interval. (In this sense it is known as a coincidence gate.)

The logic functions of the arithmetic and control units are often carried out by circuitry which uses combinations of gates. Some of these functions are:

adding binary numbers
encoding from binary to decimal or decimal to binary
comparing two numbers
counting
timing
storing the results of calculations

Each gate is a circuit, which accepts inputs in the form of a pulse (1) or a no pulse (0) and produces outputs of a pulse or a no pulse.

Logic elements are defined by what they do. They may differ in their electronic makeup.

To develop a system of two-state logic we need just three basic items of equipment or logic elements. They are represented in diagrams by symbols which are distorted forms of the arrow shown in Figure 5.2(a). This arrow is not itself used in the diagrams.

The first logic element is called an *inverter* (Figure 5.2(b)). There is one input on the left and one input on the right. The state of the output is determined by the state of the line attached to the input. If the input is high, the output is low; if the input is low, the output is high. The symbol for an inverter is sometimes drawn with the small circle at the point of the arrow.

The second logic element is called an OR gate (Figure

5.2(c)). Two inputs are shown on the left, but there could be more. One output is shown on the right. The state of the output is determined by the state of the lines attached to the inputs. If all the inputs are low, the output is low. If any one or more of the inputs is high, the output is high.

The third logic element is called an AND gate (Figure 5.2(d)). It has two or more inputs on the left and one output on the right. The state of the output is determined by the state of the lines attached to the inputs. If all the inputs are high, the output is high. If any one or more of the inputs is low, the output is low.

Very complex control systems can be built up by the use of these three logic elements. We offer a few simple diagrams.

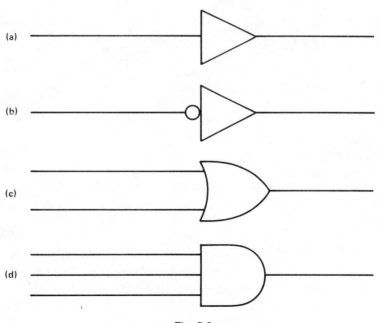

Fig. 5.2.

In Figure 5.3(a) the output of an OR gate is connected to the input of an inverter. This arrangement is called a NOR gate. The symbol for inverters can be abbreviated by omitting the inverter and attaching a small circle to the output or input of the gate to which it is connected (Figure 5.3(b)). Figure 5.4 shows three gates combined with inverters. Figure 5.5 shows two symbols, which have identical effects: (a) is called a negated input OR gate and (b) is called a NAND gate. The NOR and NAND gates are often used as the basic gates. They can be combined with inverters to produce OR and AND gates as in Figure 5.6, which is in effect an OR gate.

A truth table is a table of states existing at various points in a diagram, and in particular at the output, for all possible combinations of input states. If a diagram has only one input, it can be in the high or low state. If there are two inputs, each can be high or low so that there are four possible combinations. If there are three inputs, there are eight possible input combinations.

In general, if there are n inputs, there are 2^n possible input combinations. Figure 5.7 shows this drawn out in full and a number of points lettered. The truth table for this diagram is as follows:

A	B	C	D	E
H	H	L	H	L
L	H	L	L	H
H	L	H	H	L
L	L	H	H	L

This table is constructed by making a column for each point of interest in the diagram. These points include inputs, outputs, and a point on each connecting line between symbols. The column headings are letters which represent the points in question. The table has, in addition to the top row of letters, 2^n

rows where n is the number of inputs. There are two inputs, A and B, in Figure 5.7 and thus four rows. The columns for the inputs are filled in with all the possible combinations of H and L (high and low states). The properties of the logic elements can be used with the input columns to fill in the remaining columns of the table. In Figure 5.7, in which there are the inputs A and

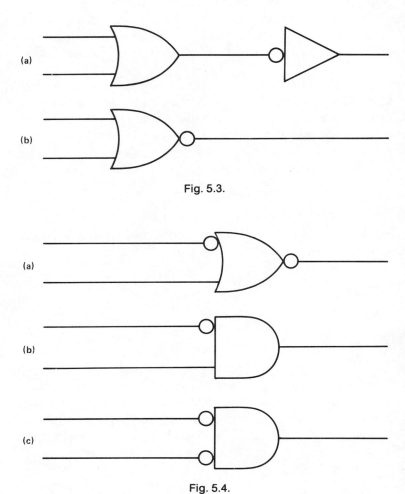

Fig. 5.3.

Fig. 5.4.

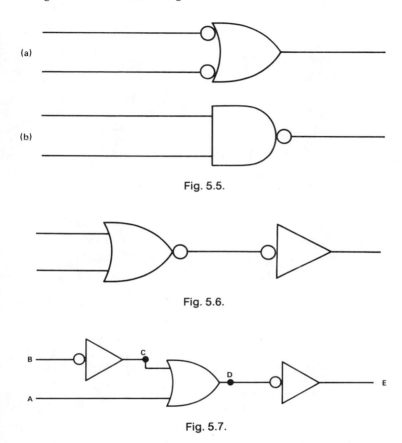

(a)

(b)

Fig. 5.5.

Fig. 5.6.

Fig. 5.7.

B, column C is obtained from column B by the use of the inverter property: if B is H, C is L; if B is L, C is H. Column D is obtained from columns A and C by using the OR gate property: if either input is H, the output is H. The inverter property is used to obtain column E from column D. If we read the rows of the truth table, we can quickly see the output state for any of the possible input states.

The flip-flop is one of the basic building blocks of the computer. Figure 5.8 shows a logic and a circuit diagram for a

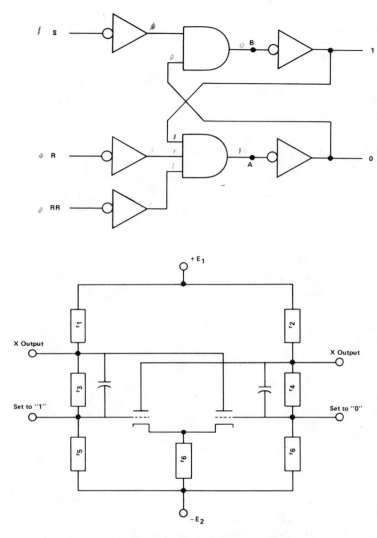

Fig. 5.8. Two basic flip-flop circuits.

58

flip-flop circuit. A flip-flop stores a binary digit, which is contracted to bit, the basic quantum of information.

There are several sets of symbols in use for the operations of Boolean algebra. Here are some selected symbols:

- ·   for AND
- +   for OR
- −   for invert (superscript bar)
- ⊕   for exclusive OR
- ≡   for equivalence

It is not our purpose here to explain the whole of Boolean algebra, but just as a sample of what Boolean equations look like, we give the laws governing the development of equations to represent logical systems.

There are three basic laws of Boolean algebra.
First, it is communicative, i.e.,

$$A + B = B + A$$
$$A.B = B.A$$

Second, it is associative, i.e.,

$$A + B + C = A + (B + C) = (A + B) + C$$
$$A.B.C = A.(B.C) = (A.B).C$$

Third, it is distributive, i.e.,

$$A.(B + C) = A.B + A.C$$
$$A + (B.C) = (A + B).(A + C)$$

These laws can be proved by truth tables. It is of interest to note that all these laws apply in ordinary algebra except for the second part of the distributive law.

chapter 6

Charles Babbage

Charles Babbage, that engaging and exasperating man, was a Moses who never got to the Promised Land. He mapped the long weary road to it up to the very gates, but it was not until more than half a century after his death that the gates were opened into the country of the computer and we could all enjoy its fruits. Some of these fruits have turned out to have a bitter taste—the computer has dislocated our jobs and invaded our privacy—but it is certain that the gates will never be closed again.

Babbage, a genius of superb capacity, industry, and integrity, had the misfortune to be ahead of the technology of his time. (See Figure 6.1.) When he conceived his computer, he had to design most of the tools to build it with. He even had to devise a method of notation to be used in his mechanical drawings. Although his computer never got off the ground, the work done on it advanced machine technology by decades.

Babbage also had the defects of his qualities. The very fertility of his genius was a hindrance to his success. He would make the drawings for parts of his difference engine and have the gears cut and a subassembly put together. Then he would think of a better design for the subassembly or some part of it, scrap the whole thing, and begin again. Since all these parts were expensively hand made, money kept going down the drain.

Fig. 6.1. (*Courtesy of IBM*)

62

Furthermore, the improvements he thought up often involved greater elaboration and complexity, so that his vision of his calculating engines, however sound in theory, was impractical for the money and time he had at his disposal.

Babbage was a short-tempered, uncompromising man who did not suffer fools gladly; he would insult the Royal Society at the same time that he was trying to get money from it. His lifetime feud with organ-grinders and street musicians has been made much of, but certainly we can sympathize with him. Street musicians provided the noise pollution of the day, and it is estimated that there were some 1,000 organ-grinders in London alone. Our radios and TVs can be turned down if the owner is sufficiently decent or intimidated. London's organs and brass bands, blaring away in a narrow street outside the house where Babbage was working, couldn't. In fact, as is true today, frequenters of pubs and the under-entertained lower classes loved loud noises and objected to any interference with this free entertainment. Thomas Carlyle resorted to a soundproof room to shut out the noise of the street musicians, but Babbage preferred to fight. At times Babbage was followed in the streets by groups of rowdies threatening to burn his house down.

Whatever his peculiarities, he must have been a most attractive man. He had hosts of friends, among them the great men of his time. He was also a family man—he had seven children. But his work was the center of his life. He said that "through life I have never hesitated to make the severest sacrifices of fortune, and even of feelings, in order to accomplish my imagined mission." That mission was to produce the prototype of the modern computer.

Babbage was born in Devonshire in 1792, the son of a banker. He was a sickly child and was sent to a school run by a clergyman "with instructions to attend to my health; but not to press too much knowledge upon me: a mission which he faithfully accomplished. Perhaps great idleness may have led to some of my childish reasonings."

At any rate Charles made numerous experiments. To find out whether there really were ghosts or whether people were just putting him on, he went to a deserted garret, cut his finger, and drew a circle around himself on the floor with the blood, then said the Lord's Prayer backward in an attempt to raise the devil.

I then stood still in the center of that magic and superstitious circle, looking with intense anxiety in all directions, especially at the window and at the chimney.... No owl or black cat or unlucky raven came into the room.

He also tried to communicate with the ghost of his best friend on the day of the friend's death, and kept a vigil in his room.

The distant clock and a faithful dog, just outside my own door, produced the only sounds which disturbed the intense silence of that anxious night.

His attempt to walk on the water almost finished him. He used the hinged covers of two old books on the soles of his shoes.

My theory was that in lifting up my leg, as in the act of walking, the two boards would close up toward each other, whilst on pushing down my foot, the water would rush between the boards, cause them to open out into a flat surface, and thus offer greater resistance to my sinking in the water.

The theory was fine, but one pair of hinges got out of order and he barely made it to shore.

In his first year at Trinity College, Cambridge, Babbage was astonished to discover that none of his instructors knew as much about calculus as he did; and also that they covered up their ignorance with various evasions. He then commenced his lifelong role as the gadfly of English education, as he was later to become the gadfly of English science.

At Cambridge, Babbage, Herschel (son of the famous astronomer) and others organized the Analytical Society. It undertook as one task the checking of celestial tables, which were published for astonomers and mariners. They were used reluctantly by the latter because they contained so many errors that a ship that used them was as likely to run on the rocks as to reach port.

A friend later reminded him of an anecdote he had himself forgotten:

> One evening I was sitting in the rooms of the Analytical Society, at Cambridge, my head leaning forward on the table in a kind of dreamy mood, with a table of logarithms lying open before me. Another member, coming into the room, and seeing me half asleep, called out, "Well, Babbage, what are you dreaming about?" to which I replied, "I am thinking that all these tables (pointing to the logarithms) might be calculated by machinery."

The idea stayed with him from that time on. His "imagined mission" had taken hold of him.

Charles graduated from Cambridge in 1814 and the same year married Georgiana Whitmore. The couple moved into the upstairs rooms of the elder Babbage's house at 5 Devonshire and Charles had a workshop above the stables. He could have become a junior partner in his father's bank, but the idea did not appeal to him.

Babbage's first publication appeared in the *Memoirs of the Analytical Society* in 1813. He soon began publishing in established journals and was invited to become a member of the Royal Society when he was still at Cambridge as a graduate student.

In 1817 the *Philosophical Transactions* published Babbage's paper, "On Some New Methods of Investigating the Sums of Several Classes of Infinite Series." Babbage wrote to a friend:

> I send you a copy of a paper of mine on functions on which subject I am decidedly mad without the remotest possibility of a cure, seeing that it is so fertile in beautiful results that it might well occupy half a dozen lives without being near exhausted. I have received some excellent remarks on them from Bromhead, who is also a little touched.

It was logical enough for Babbage to turn away from mathematical theory to the development of a tool that would produce these "beautiful results" without occupying half a dozen lives. As a beginning he began to collect the calculators so far devised, but none of them satisfied him.

> I considered that a machine to execute the mere isolated operations of arithmetic would be comparatively of little value, unless it were very easily set to do its work, and unless it executed not only accurately, but with great rapidity, whatever it was required to do.
> On the other hand, the method of differences supplied a general principle by which all tables might be computed through limited intervals, by one uniform process. Again, the method of differences required the use of mechanism for addition only. In order, however, to insure accuracy in the printed tables, it was necessary that the machine which computed tables should also set them up in type, or else supply a mould in which stereotype plates of those tables could be cast.

Babbage made use of Stanhope's arithmetic machines. The first idea of an automatic calculator employing functional differences has been attributed to J. H. Müller in 1786. It is not certain whether Babbage knew of Müller's work, but he never gave any credit, at least in writing, to Müller.

Babbage noted that his difference engine is not intended to answer special questions, but to calculate and print a series of results formed according to given laws—that is, tables. Babbage illustrated the concept by a table of the price of meat at 5d. (5 pence) per pound:

Number lbs.	Price s.	d.
1	0	5
2	0	10
3	1	3
4	1	8
5	2	1

If we express this table in pence, we see that its first difference is a constant and equal to 5:

Number lbs.	Price d.	1st Difference
1	5	
2	10	5
3	15	5
4	20	5
5	25	5

Any machine, therefore, which could add one number to another, and at the same time retain the original number called the first difference for the next operation, would be able to compute all such tables.

In more complicated tables the first difference is not a constant amount, and. it is necessary to go to a second difference—or further—before a constant difference is arrived at. A table of squares would be as follows:

x Number	$x^2 = x.x$ Square	1st Difference	2nd Difference
1	1		
2	4	3	—
3	9	5	2
4	16	7	2
5	25	9	2

Babbage refers his reader to the heaps of cannon balls in the arsenal at Portsmouth. Successive sizes of triangular pyramids of these balls work out to a table with three differences:

Order Number	No. of Balls	1st Difference	2nd Difference	3rd Difference
1	1			
2	4	3		
3	10	6	3	—
4	20	10	4	1
5	35	15	5	1
6	56	21	6	1

The addition of a printing mechanism greatly increased the complexity and cost of the machine, of course, since at that time there were no automatic typesetting machines and Babbage had to design his own.

To produce a table of squares on Babbage's machine the operator would set a 1 on the wheel of the number column, a 3 on the first difference column, and a 2 on the second difference column. The first turn of the wheel would print a 1. The second turn of the wheel would add 3 to the 1 to make 4, and at the same time add 2 to the 3 to make 5 on the first difference column. The next turn of the wheel would print 4 plus 5, or 9. And so on.

Babbage set about to construct a model. When his own mechanical abilities were no longer up to the work, he employed a wheel-cutter. His plans for the printer called for 30,000 pieces of movable type, locked to preclude mistakes in typesetting. He also experimented with printing from type permanently affixed to the computing wheels. Printing was to be done on paper, copper plates, or plaster of Paris molds.

Babbage's first experimental model had 96 computing wheels mounted on 24 shafts. He then made a simpler version with 18 wheels on three shafts, but this could calculate only two orders of difference. Each turn of the handle would transfer the number on each shaft to the shaft on the left of it by means of toothed gears. A carry lever actuated a wheel above when a total reached 10 or more. (See Figure 6.2.)

Babbage now needed only money to produce a complete full-scale model. One possibility was the new Astronomical Society. Its *Memoirs* for June 1822 published his "Note Respecting the Application of Machinery to the Calculation of Math-

Fig. 6.2. Part of Babbage's Difference Engine. (*Courtesy of IBM*)

ematical Tables," and he explained his difference engine at a meeting of the society. The members were so impressed that the society gave him its first gold medal.

However, the Royal Society was the organization best able to help him, and in July he wrote to its president, Sir Humphrey Davy:

> The intolerable labor and fatiguing monotony of a continued repetition of similar arithmetical calculations first excited the desire, and afterwards suggested the idea, of a machine, which, by the aid of gravity or any other moving power, should become a substitute for one of the lowest operations of human intellect.

At Davy's urging an unwritten agreement was made that the chancellor of the exchequer would supply Babbage with funds for a difference engine. The first grant was for £1,500, and the total cost was estimated at between £3,000 and £5,000. Babbage was to donate his services. The vagueness of the agreement caused later problems concerning who owned the difference engine, and whether the the government was supposed to underwrite the whole project. Neither party had a true concept of the project. It would have cost some 50 times more money than was estimated and would have needed about two tons of specially made clockwork. These parts could not even be made by the tools then in existence, so the project would have had to pull along behind it in the development of the mechanic arts. Undismayed by the prospect, Babbage set out with his £1,500 to build an engine that would calculate to six orders of difference and 20 places of accuracy.

Babbage's calculators were by no means his only interest. He did research and wrote papers in many fields, sometimes on his own, sometimes as a paid consultant. He suggested a screw-propelled submarine and a rocket system to boost projectiles. He devised a system of occulting signals for lighthouses, which was tried and favorably reported upon by the U. S. Lighthouse Board.

Babbage published more than 80 papers on subjects ranging from magnetization during rotation to archaeology and astronomy. His successful book, *Economy of Manufactures*, pioneered in the science of operations research. He proposed that a flat rate be charged for postage instead of a rate based on distance, and thus instigated the Penny Post. He was interested in picking locks and in making locks proof against picking; in devising codes and in cracking them. He investigated actuarial satistics for a prospective insurance company, and produced a set of what were probably the first reliable insurance tables. As a consultant on railroad building to the engineer Isambard Kingdom Brunel he carefully graphed the motions of railroad cars. Babbage also made various safety suggestions, such as a semaphore signal, a device for separating a derailed engine from a train, and a cowcatcher:

[E]very engine should have just in advance of each of its front wheels a powerful framing, supporting a strong piece of plate-iron, descending within an inch or two of the upper face of the rail. These iron plates should be fixed at an angle of 45° with the line of rail, and also at the same angle with respect to the horizon. Their shape would be somewhat like that of ploughshares, and their effect would be to pitch any obstacle obliquely off the rail unless its heavier portion were between the rails.

Meanwhile, what of the difference engine? The original appropriation ran out, and a new application for funds was approved in 1828. The government was also to build a fireproof building and workshop on land leased next to Babbage's home.

In 1827 Babbage lost his father, two of his children, and his wife. It was small consolation that on the death of his father he inherited some half-million dollars. He fell ill—probably more sick at heart than otherwise—and at the insistence of his mother and his doctor he left the country for a year's rest. In Europe he studied the operation of machines, including spinning frames and looms, and visited menageries to pursue his researches on the pulse and breathing rate of animals. A high—or low—point of his trip was his descent into the crater of Vesuvius, which he accomplished with the aid of ropes and a final free slide. With scientific calm, he observed the increasingly larger succession of bubbles, or vesicles, boiling up in the lava. Finally prudence prevailed.

> I would gladly have remained a longer time, but the excessive heat, the noxious vapors, and the warning of my chronometer forbade it. I climbed back through the gap by which I had descended, and rushed as fast as I could to a safe distance from the coming eruption. I was much exhausted by the heat, although I suffered still greater inconvenience from the vapors .... On my return to Naples I found that a pair of thick boots I had worn on this expedition were entirely destroyed by the heat, and fell to pieces in my attempt to take them off.

In Rome Babbage learned that he had finally been elected to the Lucasian professorship at Cambridge. This was the chair of Newton, and it was, he said later, the only honor he ever received from his own country. He returned to England in 1829. A little more money was forthcoming from the exchequer, and work resumed on the difference engine. But in 1833 the project ground to a halt. Babbage's engineer, Clement, refused to move the engine to the new shops but held it as security, claiming that he and his workmen had not been paid on time. He refused to continue work without new and expensive arrangements. The government suspended payments.

A settlement was finally arrived at by which the drawings and parts were to be moved to the new building. But Clement was the legal owner of his tools, although they had been paid for with money from Babbage and the government. Babbage ruefully noted that Clement, who had started out with one lathe and a workshop in his kitchen, now had tools worth several thousand pounds and a converted chapel for a workshop. And Joseph Whitworth, another associate, had become the greatest toolmaker in England and been knighted.

Babbage had part of the calculating section of the engine —all he could assemble—put together, and it worked perfectly. If he had been content with a less ambitious design, he might have finished his engine within the allotted funds and time.

The ruin of his difference engine lay around his feet. A lesser man might have had thoughts of suicide.

Instead Babbage immediately started the design of another and far more powerful calculator, the analytical engine. It would be able to carry out any mathematical operation, not just the routine of differences.

The part of the difference engine that he had assembled performed far beyond his original expectations. One extra potential was that, if a few more connecting gears were added, the result produced in the last column of gears could be fed back to other points in the engine.

Babbage now hit upon the idea of arranging his analytical engine, not in line, but with the axes around a central shaft. Output would thus be close to input. The engine could then, as he put it, bite its own tail, and control itself. A result produced by the machine could be used to retrieve further information from the store, and this information could be fed into the mill. (Although in the United States we talk about the computer memory and the arithmetic unit, in Britain the memory is still called the store.)

Thus the concept of the modern computer was born. Babbage now extended his scheme of mechanical notation to take care of the complications of the new machine.* He hired workmen, at high wages since the railroad mania had absorbed the best draftsmen.

---

* The modern drafstman may be interested in four conventions established by Babbage in his system of notation:

One piece may be driven by another in such a manner that when the driver moves, the other also always moves; as happens when a wheel is driven by a pinion. } An arrow without any bar. ⟶

Numbers had been entered in the difference engine by hand. Babbage now hit upon the idea of using Jacquard's punched cards to enter them. He explained:

The Analytical Engine consists of two parts:
1st. The store in which all the variables to be operated upon, as well as all those quantities which have arisen from the result of other operations, are placed.
2nd. The mill into which the quantities about to be operated upon are always brought.

Every formula which the Analytical Engine can be required to compute consists of certain algebraical operations to be performed upon given letters, and of certain other modification depending on the numerical value assigned to those letters.

There are therefore two sets of cards, the first to direct the nature of the operations to be performed—these are called operation cards: the other to direct the particular variables on which those cards are required to operate—these latter are called variable cards. Now the symbol of each variable or constant is placed at the top of a column capable of containing any required number of digits.

Under this arrangement, when any formula is required to be computed, a set of operation cards must be strung together, which contains the series of operations in the order in which they occur. Another set of cards must then be strung together, to call in the variables into the mill, in the order in which they are required to be acted upon. Each operation card will require three other cards, two to represent the variables and constants and their numerical values upon which the previous operation card is to act, and one to indicate the variable on which the arithmetical result of this operation is to be placed.

One thing may be attached to another by stiff friction. } An arrow formed of a line interrupted by dots.
—.—.—.—.—.—.➤

One piece may be driven by another, and yet not always move when the latter moves; as is the case when a stud lifts a bolt once in the course of its revolution. } By an arrow, the first half of which is a full line, and the second half a dotted one.
——— ......➤

One wheel may be connected with another by a ratchet, as the great wheel of a clock is attached to the fusee. } By a dotted arrow with a ratchet tooth at its end.
.ʌ..............➤

Babbage noted that the analytical engine was therefore a machine of the most general nature. The cards were reusable —every set of cards made for any formula would at any future time recalculate that formula with whatever constants were wanted. The analytical engine would thus have a library of its own.

If the machine needed some formula, such as a logarithm, that was not in its store, it would ring a bell and then stop itself, and an attendant would fetch the number.

Babbage proposed a machine that would be able to express every number it used to 50 places. He estimated that 60 additions or subtractions could be done and printed in one minute, and multiplication and division in comparable times.

The analytical engine would print out its results on paper or metal plates, or produce a stereotype mold for printing multiple copies. It would also have a device for punching holes in cards. Babbage's cards had eleven rows and nine holes in each row. He succeeded in devising a mechanism for high-speed carry. The store would hold only 1,000 50-digit numbers, but these could be replaced to increase the capacity of the machine.

The analytical engine was a truly marvelous concept. But when Babbage presented it to the government, he got a cold turndown. It was plain that if he wanted to build it, he would have to do it without their help. He decided to go it alone with his own money.

Babbage's friend, the Italian General M. Menabrea, first brought the analytical engine to public notice in 1842 by publishing an explanation of it in a journal. The Countess of Lovelace translated this paper, and at Babbage's suggestion she added extensive notes of her own.

Babbage's friendship with the young Ada Lovelace, the only child of Lord Byron, was a source of great pleasure to him. She was a gifted mathematician, and her husband, the first Earl of Lovelace, encouraged her in her work. Ada was one of the few to appreciate Babbage's calculating engines. On a visit to see

Directive Card	*Operation Card*	—
1st	—	Places *a* on column 1 of Store
2nd	—	Places *b* on column 2 of Store
3rd	—	Places *c* on column 3 of Store
4th	—	Places *d* on column 4 of Store
5th	—	Brings *a* from Store to Mill
6th	—	Brings *b* from Store to Mill
—	1	Multiplies *a* and *b* = *p*
7th	—	Takes *p* to column 5 of Store where it is kept for use and record
8th	—	Brings *p* into Mill
9th	—	Brings *c* into Mill
—	2	Adds *p* and *c* = *q*
10th	—	Takes *q* to column 6 of Store
11th	—	Brings *d* into Mill
12th	—	Brings *q* into Mill
—	3	Multiplies *d* × *q* = p_2
13th	—	Takes p_2 to column 7 of Store
14th	—	Takes p_2 to printing or stereo-moulding apparatus

Fig. 6.3. Cards for Babbage's Analytical Engine. Cards for (ab + c) d.

Babbage's work, the friend who accompanied her described her reaction:

> While the rest of the party gazed at this beautiful instrument with the same sort of expression and feeling that some savages are said to have shown on first seeing a looking glass or hearing a gun, Miss Byron, young as she was, understood its working and saw the great beauty of the invention.

Ada discerned one of the most important abilities of the machine:

The engine is capable, under certain circumstances, of feeling about to discover which of two or more possible contingencies has occurred, and of shaping its future course of action accordingly.

Babbage had hoped that he would have another young protégé in his son Henry, but Henry preferred the military service and in 1843 left for India.

The Lovelaces and Babbage were racing fans, and Babbage tried to devise a mathematical scheme for predicting the winners. Ada became obsessed with the scheme and gambled compulsively, then became ill and died in 1852, when she was 36. Babbage felt in some part responsible for the tragedy.

Babbage never produced a complete prototype of the analytical engine, but two other men copied parts of his designs. A Londoner named Deacon made a small model of the calculating part of the difference engine, but it was shown only to a few friends. George Scheutz, a printer in Sweden, utilized the difference engine to design a kind of automatic typesetting machine that could also prepare mathematical tables. Scheutz, neither a mathematician nor a machine designer, had a good deal of trouble.

Scheutz's difference engine was more ambitious than Babbage's demonstration model of 1822. It computed four orders of differences to 14 places and printed the results automatically. Sweden gave Scheutz several grants, and he had the help of his son and the support of many members of the Swedish Academy. (See Figure 6.5.)

Scheutz took his engine to England in 1854, and Babbage and Henry generously made up drawings and mechanical notation to explain its operation, and helped to promote it. Scheutz's machine received a gold medal in the 1855 Exhibition in Paris, where Babbage's engine was not even shown.

The Scheutz machine was bought in 1854 for the Dudley Observatory at Albany, and became the first automatic computer to operate in the United States. It was used to print

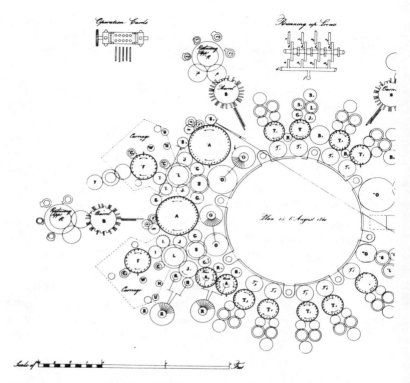

Fig. 6.4. Babbage's Analytical Engine. (Halacy, *Charles Babbage*)

astronomical tables. An exact copy of the Scheutz machine was later made for the English government and was used to compute actuarial tables, which eventually superseded the tables Babbage had constructed in 1826.

Another imitator of Babbage was George Barnard Grant, whose chief interest in life was gears. He was a successful manufacturer of them—his *Gears* is a classic work and can still be bought. Among the companies he founded were the Grant Gear Works, the Philadelphia Gear Works, and the Boston Gear Works.

Grant was born in Maine in 1849 and got his B. S. from

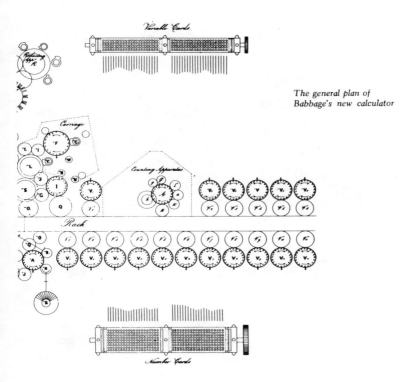

The general plan of
Babbage's new calculator

Harvard in 1873. He was interested in calculators before he
heard about Babbage and Scheutz, and when he became
acquainted with Babbage's work, started to build his own
calculator. He developed a calculating section and a printing
section. The printer produced a stereotyped plate.

Grant's ambition was to build a better and simpler machine
than the arithmometer of Charles Xavier Thomas—one the
ordinary man could operate and maintain. Most people in the
United States were not familiar with Babbage's work, and
Grant's ideas were an innovation. He built his calculator for the
1876 Centennial Exhibition; it was 8 feet long and 5 feet high,
weighed 2,000 pounds, and had 15,000 parts.

Whatever the difficulties with his calculators, Babbage was

Fig. 6.5. George Scheutz's Calculator. (*Courtesy of IBM*)

a highly productive scientist in many fields, and it is hard to understand the indifference and even animosity shown him by the government and the public. He was an authority on industry, yet he was not asked to help in planning the Exhibition of 1851 in the Crystal Palace, or to exhibit in it. His request to put what remained of his difference engine in the British Museum was denied. The government instead buried it at King's College, and refused to disinter it when it was requested for exhibition in Dublin and New York.

Babbage's difference engine was at last displayed at the Exhibition of 1862. Babbage offered to display the drawings of the engine too, and to lend his collection of calculating engines for the exhibition. He was refused on both counts. After the exhibition King's College did not want the difference engine back, and it was sent to the South Kensington Museum. It is still there.

In 1864 Babbage published his autobiography. In the preface he says:

Some men write their lives to save themselves from ennui, careless of the amount they inflict on their readers. Others write their personal history, lest some kind friend should survive them, and, in showing off his own talent, unwittingly show them up. Others, again, write their own life from a different motive—from fear that the vampires of literature might make it their prey.

Babbage wrote to preserve some account of the history of his calculators, and leavened the account with his personal reminiscences.

Babbage died when he was close to 80. Except for his family, there was only one mourner at his funeral.

He left what there was of his engines to his son Henry. In 1874 Henry retired from the military, and spent the next five years on the difference engine. However, the machine work was so expensive that he gave up. In 1879 he started working on the mill and printing section of the analytical engine. At last, on January 21, 1888, he turned the crank of the mill, and the printing machine produced a table of the multiples of pi to 39 places. At the 22nd multiple, however, trouble developed in the carriage and a wrong number was printed. In 1906 Henry finally debugged the carriage and had the engine modified accordingly. By that time he had given the analytical engine to the South Kensington Museum.

Charles Babbage made a prediction about his work:

The great principles on which the Analytical Engine rests have been examined, admitted, recorded, and demonstrated. The mechanism itself has now been reduced to unexpected simplicity. Half a century may probably elapse before any one without those aids which I leave behind me, will attempt so unpromising a task. If, unwarned by my example, any man shall undertake and shall succeed in really constructing an engine embodying in itself the whole of the executive department of

mathematical analysis upon different principles or by simpler mechanical means, I have no fear of leaving my reputation in his charge,
for he alone will be fully able to appreciate the nature of my efforts and
the value of their results.

chapter 7

Key-Driven Calculators

Pascal and his successors entered numbers in their calculators by hand. Babbage used hand entry in his difference engine, and went to punched cards for his analytical engine.

Would-be inventors soon sought some faster means of data entry and many of them thought of the use of depressible keys, such as actuated the piano. But this was a harder problem than it seemed.

Two keyboard types of machines developed. In the key-driven type the energy to drive the machine was provided by the depression of the figure keys; in the key-setting type it was supplied by the depression of a handle after the figure keys were set. The difficulty with both types was that the actuating force was not constant and neither was its effect, and errors were probable.

In 1850 D. D. Parmelee got a patent for a key-driven adding machine. (See Figure 7.1.) In place of numeral wheels it had a long ratchet-toothed bar, numbered on the flat faces. Control was by means of spring-loaded ratchet pawls. The operator of the Parmelee machine would have had to use a keystroke light as a zephyr or the numerical bar would overshoot and give a wrong answer since there was no provision for overcoming the momentum imparted to the numeral bar in an add stroke.

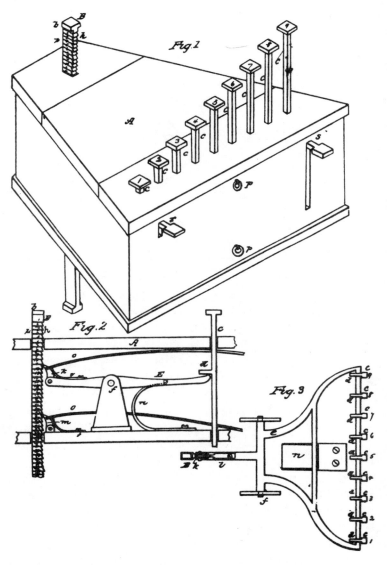

Fig. 7.1. Parmelee calculator. (J. A. V. Turck, *Origin of Modern Calculating Machines*)

A number of key-driven machines were made between 1851 and 1887. Like Parmelee's, they could add only a single column of digits at a time. It was necessary to add the units first and note the total; then to clear the machine and add the carry figures to the next column. The competition to this type of machine was the trained human being, who was faster.

The next hurdle was to make the key-driven machine do what the machines of Pascal and his successors could do—add a number of columns, say six or eight, at the same time in a multiple-order machine. In 1857 Thomas Hill got a patent on a multiple-order key-driven machine. (See Figure 7.2.) This invention got a good deal of undeserved publicity because the Patent Office model was exhibited in the National Museum at Washington. However, as one writer comments:

> The functions of the Hill mechanism would, perhaps, be practical if it were not for the physical law that bodies set in motion tend to remain in motion .... The feature lacking was a means for controlling the action of the mechanism under the tremendously increased speed produced by the use of depressible keys as an actuating means.... Imagine the sudden whirl his numeral wheel would receive on a quick depression of a key and then consider that he provided no means for stopping these wheels.

The writer adds that "perchance Hill thought the operator of his machine could mentally control the wheels against over-rotation." He concludes that it is as much an error to call the Hill device an adding machine as to call the Langley aeroplane a flying machine; the one could not add, and the other could not fly.

In 1872 Robjohn patented a single-digit adding machine that did have a stop device to prevent overrotation of the units wheel, though there was nothing to prevent the overflow of the higher, or tens, wheels in the event of a carry.

M. Bouchet made the first attempt to control the carried wheel in 1882, using a Geneva gear to lock the wheel. The

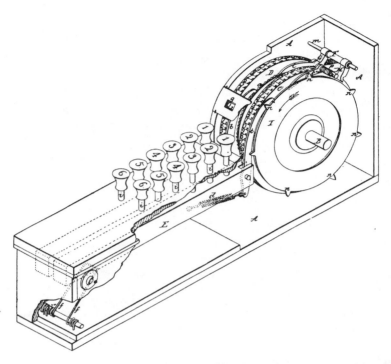

Fig. 7.2. Patent drawing for Hill's multiple-order key-driven machine. (J. A. V. Turck, *Origin of Modern Calculating Machines*)

Bouchet single-order machine was manufactured and some units were sold, but it never became popular.

Dorr E. Felt and the Comptometer

It was 30 years before an operative multiple-order key-driven machine was invented by Dorr E. Felt, a young machinist. The adjustable ratchet feed on a planer suggested to him a solution of the calculator problem. Felt realized that a practical machine must work faster than the average expert accountant, who could add four columns of figures at a time.`

Therefore I worked on the principle of duplicate denominational orders that could be stretched to any capacity within reason. The plan I finally settled on is displayed in what is generally known as the Macaroni Box model. This crude model was made under rather adverse circumstances.

The construction of such a complicated machine from metal, as I had schemed up, was not within my reach from a monetary standpoint, so I decided to put my ideas into wood.

It was near Thanksgiving Day of 1884, and I decided to use the holiday in the construction of the wooden model. I went to the grocer's and selected a box which seemed to me to be about the right size for the casing. It was a macaroni box, so I have always called it the macaroni box model. For keys I procured some meat skewers from the butcher around the corner and some staples from a hardware store for the key guides and an assortment of elastic bands to be used for springs. When Thanksgiving day came I got up early and went to work with a few tools, principally a jackknife.

I soon discovered that there were some parts which would require better tools than I had at hand for the purpose, and when night came I found that the model I had expected to construct in a day was a long way from being complete or in working order. I finally had some of the parts made out of metal, and finished the model soon after New Year's day, 1885.

The Comptometer was born.

Felt was the first to really solve the problem of a controlled carrying mechanism. Such a mechanism must (1) store power to perform the carry; (2) unlock the numeral wheel to be carried; (3) deliver the stored power to the carrying operation; (4) stop and lock the carried wheel when the carry has been registered; (5) clear the carrying lock when another cycle is to be performed. Felt, like his predecessors, used a combination of springs, ratchets, pawls, cams, detents, and catches, but he made them work. One of the more important features of the device was the timing of the stop and locking detents.

Felt started to make his calculator himself in 1886. (See Figure 7.3.) Since he had little money, he had to make the machines himself. One of them was bought by the Registrar of the Treasury, and put to constant use. In 1887, with Robert Tarrant of Chicago, Felt formed the Felt & Tarrant Mfg. Co. Their Comptometer was to preempt the market for the next 15 years.

The Comptometer's value was enhanced by the schemes Felt developed for its use. He supplied his customers with detailed instructions for the four basic operations and also for square and cube root, interest, discount, exchange, English currency, and so forth.

Felt soon devised a recorder to go with his calculator, but his first model was hand wound and could not print zeros. His second was successful. Each figure was visibly printed as the key was depressed. The paper was advanced by a hand lever on the

Fig. 7.3. Felt's "macaroni box." (*Courtesy of IBM*)

right-hand side, and the action of this lever stored the power for the printing so that it was not necessary to wind a spring by hand.

Printing mechanisms now received attention from other designers, one of them Frank S. Baldwin, who secured a patent in 1875. The Baldwin machine incorporates the system found in the machines known as the Brunsviga (Figure 7.4), made under the Odhner patents—a later foreign invention used extensively abroad. Baldwin's innovation seems to be only the roll of paper ribbon and the ink ribbon.

The Pottin machine for recording cash transactions was patented in 1883. It was the first known machine operated by depressible keys and a crank that could add columns of figures; it was the first to print numerical items as they were added. Printing was on a roll of paper or on a separate bill.

The Cash Register and NCR

In 1878 James Ritty, a restaurant owner en route to Europe on an ocean liner, watched the operation of a gauge that counted the number of revolutions of the propeller. He decided

Fig. 7.4. Brunsviga Trinks. (*Courtesy of IBM*)

that a similar machine could be developed to record the transactions in his business.

When he got home, he went to work with his brother John on what was to become the first cash register. The first model had two rows of keys and a large clocklike dial containing two rows of figures. The keys controlled the hands, which showed dollars and cents on the dial. A later model was called Ritty's Incorruptible Cashier.

The first cash register marketed was the paper roll machine. Since there was no adding-disk mechanism, James Ritty mounted a wide paper roll horizontally above the keys. Each key operated a sharp pin; when a key was depressed, the pin would pierce a hole in the roll of paper in the proper column; the paper roll would then advance. At the end of the day, the proprietor would remove the roll of paper and count the holes in each column. Ten holes in the 5-cent column showed he had done a 50-cent business in 5-cent sales.

The machines sold poorly, and Ritty sold the business to Jacob H. Eckert for $1,000. In 1882 Eckert organized The National Manufacturing Company. At about this time the cash drawer and the bell were added.

The next owner of the business was John H. Patterson, who finally got the business going. He changed the name to the National Cash Register Company. Patterson's first factory was 40 feet wide and 80 feet long and he had 13 employees. The output was four or five registers a week. (See Figure 7.5.) Today NCR has some 95,000 employees and factories in 10 countries.

Patterson was a pioneer in sales procedures and training. His theory was that the best way to sell is to help the customer recognize and solve the problems in his own business. Now NCR is the world's second largest producer of general business equipment. It manufactures general business machines, data terminals, computers, and adding machines.

The First Cash Register

The Paper Roll Machine

The Detail Adders

The Total Adder

The Detail Audit-Strip

The Receipt Printer

Triple Printer

Class 2000

Fig. 7.5. (*Courtesy of The National Cash Register Company*)

William S. Burroughs

William Seward Burroughs was born in Rochester in 1857. His first job was in a bank. Five years of adding and checking figures were enough for him, psychologically and physically. He went to St. Louis and found work in a machine shop.

He was intrigued by Felt's adding machine, his years in the bank having taught him how useful such a machine could be, and decided to design one himself. He approached Thomas Metcalf and the two got $700 together. Burroughs wanted a machine that would record entries on paper and add them progressively with a running total so that pressing a special key would provide a instant printout of the total at any time.

His first machine didn't work and his backers gave up. Burroughs persisted on his own and built 50 copies of one model, but they didn't work properly either. Operating the machine was more an art than a science; the operator had to learn to pull the lever at just the right speed or the machine would make a mistake, and Burroughs himself was the only one to master this art and get accurate results. He called back all 50 machines and destroyed them, then shut himself in his work-room to debug the device. He finally hit upon the dashpot as an automatic governor to control the effect of the lever action. The dashpot was in this instance a metal cup filled with oil in which a plunger was actuated to absorb the shock of the lever action.

In 1886 the American Arithmometer Company was formed by Burroughs, Metcalf and R. M. Scruggs (his former backers), and a new investor, W. R. Pye. Metcalf was president and Burroughs vice-president.

The next problem was to sell the product. The price of the first adding and listing machine was $475. About a quarter of a million dollars was spent before the venture got off the ground, but then it was firmly airborne. The company built up world-wide facilities for manufacture and marketing. Banks were the first marketing targets; when magnetic ink recording equipment was devised, Burroughs infiltrated the banks with it too—including the E-13B type font, which is such a nuisance to read.

(The initial impetus supplied by Burroughs has carried his company out into space; Burroughs computers have guided Gemini flights. Burroughs died in 1898, and in 1905 the company became the Burroughs Adding Machine Company. After World War II it moved to computers. Its 1950 Sensimatic Accounting Machine was the forerunner of the E-101, an electronic machine with programmed control panels and a Sensimatic for input-output. The first major Burroughs digital computer was built in 1951 for the Wayne University Computation Laboratory. In 1953 the company became the Burroughs Corporation, and in 1956 it acquired the Electro-Data Corporation, makers of general-purpose, high-speed digital computers, and Burroughs got a SAGE contract. The first ground guidance computer for Atlas missiles was delivered in 1957.

Bookkeeping Machines

Leon Bollée made the first successful direct multiplying machine, which he patented in 1889. (Figure 7.6.) His original design was made to help his father, a bell founder, in design calculations for large bells.

A machine designed by Barbour had used 18 multiplying gear racks for each order. Bollée used only two gear racks for each order, one for adding the units and the other for adding the tens. The racks could be moved in degrees corresponding to the multiplying racks in the Barbour multiplier; Bollée called them his "mechanical multiplication tables."

Fig. 7.6. Leon Bollée's machine. (*Courtesy of IBM*)

Fig. 7.7. The Millionaire. (*Courtesy of IBM*)

Bollée's machine was never manufactured, but the principle was used by a Swiss manufacturer in a nonrecording machine called The Millionaire. (See Figure 7.7.) Steiger had the U. S. patents of this machine. Hopkins used the same principle in the recording Moon-Hopkins Bookkeeping Machine, but simplified the device.

chapter 8

Punched Cards

Another tributary of the computer mainstream is the development of punched cards. It arises from an ancient source, the loom, assumed to be an early Neolithic invention.

In simple weaving, the weft or filling is passed over and under the warp threads by hand. The first way to speed this process is to thread alternate warp threads through two bars, or heddles, which can be alternately raised and lowered to form a space, or shed, through which the weft is passed. Two heddles produce a plain weave. In twill weave the warp is divided into at least three systems.

A further complication is necessary when the weaver wants to produce a pattern. This is done by the drawloom, which can vary the number and position of the warp threads to be raised for successive passes of the shuttle. The weaving of pictures with colored threads probably began in China. At some stage a pattern drawn on paper was used to guide the weavers. The paper was later ruled in squares to show the crossing of the warp and weft threads, and the pattern was marked by punched holes.

The drawloom, apparently used in Italy during the Middle Ages, had two systems for shedding. In one the weaver operated treadles. In the other there was a figure-harness above the loom from which hung cords with loops at the bottom and through which weighted warp threads were threaded. Pulling on a cord raised a thread. The cords were grouped according to the pattern to be woven. A drawboy sat on top of the loom and worked these cords by hand. He was an uncertain appurtenance; his perch was precarious and he was liable to make mistakes.

France was the leader in fancy weaving, and in 1600 a Lyons weaver, Claude Dangon, brought the cords down to the side of the machine and made the drawboy's position more secure. He also added a lever for lifting the weights on the warp. An assistant selected the cords to be raised according to a paper pattern.

In 1725 Basil Bouchon, also of Lyons, used an endless belt of punched paper for automatically selecting the cords to be pulled. Needles attached to the upper ends of the lifting cords could slide horizontally in a box. Their ends pressed against the paper tape, and the needles opposite the holes in the tape could move, their cords then lifting the corresponding warp threads. The other needles remained stationary. The pattern could thus be duplicated without error and faster than by a drawboy. The paper tape was advanced at intervals. Bouchon's device was in fact the first stored-program paper-tape machine controller, although an operator was needed to work the foot treadle that drew up the selected cords.

Three years later Falcon used several rows of needles side by side, and instead of paper tape, went to stiff cards that could be fastened together flexibly and advanced like a roll of paper.

In 1745 Jacques de Vaucanson added his touch by mounting the selecting box on the loom so that the loom could be operated from a single position and thus need fewer operators. However, his device was too complex to be practical.

Joseph Marie Jacquard

As a drawboy in a Lyons textile mill, Jacquard was considered inattentive and inefficient. He was also apprenticed in bookbinding, type founding, and cutlery. When his father died and left him a little house and a hand loom, he spent his spare time trying to improve the weaving process. In 1792 he joined the revolutionists and helped in the defense of Lyons. After he left the army, he worked on weaving improvements again in quarters supplied by the Council of Lyons, and won a prize offered by the London Society of Arts for a machine for making fishnets. The Conservatorium of Arts in Paris asked him to study one of Vaucanson's looms stored with them, and he used the design as the basis for his own loom.

In 1801 he demonstrated a new drawloom at the Paris Industrial Exhibition, and in 1805 introduced what is now called the Jacquard loom. (See Figure 8.1.) His innovation was an automatic selective device mounted on top of the loom and operated by a treadle. Instead of threading the lifting cords through needles, he used a wire with a hook in the bottom to pick up the cord and a hook at the top to fit around the griff, or lifting mechanism. Each hook passed perpendicularly through a horizontal spring-loaded needle protruding through a frame. Any hook thrust aside by the needle would miss the bars of the griff and would not lift the corresponding warp thread. The needles pressed against the perforated cards, each representing one throw of the shuttle. The pattern was transferred to the cards from the designer's sketch. (Figure 8.2.)

In 1806 Napoleon Bonaparte made Jacquard's loom public property. Jacquard got a pension and a royalty, and was made a Chevalier of the Legion of Honor. However, the weavers of the time were afraid of inventions that might cost them their jobs. Some time before in England the Luddites had broken up looms that made stockings, and now the weavers in France turned on Jacquard—at one point he barely escaped with his life.

Progress won out. When Jacquard died, in 1834, over 30,000 of his looms were in use in Lyons alone. The Jacquard machine did not appear in quantity in England until the 1820s, when an English improvement made the loom compact enough to be used in the cottage industry.

Fig. 8.1. A common handloom mounted with a 400-needle Jacquard, such as was used for the production of figured silk for gentlemen's scarves. Note belt of punched cards. (*Courtesy of Henry Carey Baird & Co.*)

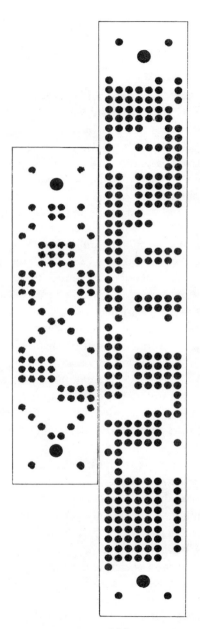

Fig. 8.2. Punched cards for a Jacquard loom. (Courtesy of Philadelphia College of Textiles and Science)

101

Herman Hollerith

Babbage was the first designer to pick up Jacquard's punched cards. Dr. Herman Hollerith was the second. Hollerith studied Jacquard's card controller, which included a card cutter, a Dobby card punching machine for punching a number of cards by a single stroke, a piano card stamping machine, and a pattern card machine for larger cards. Cards were laced together by hand or by machine.

After Hollerith graduated from the Columbia School of Mines in 1879, he got a job with the Census Bureau. When the tenth decennial census was taken in 1880, the country had grown to 50 million people, and five years later the Census Bureau was still struggling to compile the results. It was not hard to foresee a situation where a given census would not be published before it was time to take the next one.

Hollerith started work on a machine for mechanically tabulating population and other statistics, inspired by watching a conductor punch tickets with a basic description of each passenger. He left the Census Bureau to teach at MIT, but continued his experiments. In 1884 he took a job with the Patent Office, and the same year applied for his first patent on a machine for counting population statistics. He was eventually issued 31 patents.

Hollerith's most important innovations were the sensing of the holes through electrical contacts and the design of electrically operated mechanisms for incrementing the proper register in the tabulating machine. He also provided for one step in an electric sort. Each card was coded to fall into the proper pocket in a sorting box. From this point on sorting had to be done by hand, but it was easier to sort punched cards than handwritten cards because the sorter could sight through the wanted hole or use a sorting needle.

The first machine designed by Hollerith used a roll of

paper, but for the 1890 census he proposed the use of manila cards. The early census card was 6⅝ by 3¼ inches and had 24 columns, each with 12 punching places. Today's standard IBM card measures 7⅜ by 3¼ inches and has 80 columns, each with 12 punching places.

In 1889 a committee was appointed to consider the means of tabulation to be used in the 1890 census. Three systems were tested, one of them Hollerith's. (See Figure 8.3.) His system took only about two-thirds as long as its nearest competitor to transcribe information. Its biggest advantage was in tabulating; its electric counters tabulated the test data in 5 hours and 28 minutes. Hollerith's machine was in. The commission estimated that on a basis of 65,000,000 population, the Hollerith machine would save almost $600,000.

Hollerith subcontracted the development of his device for mass production—the keypunch to Pratt & Whitney and the tabulator to Western Electric. He described his system:

> Data cards were punched with holes on spots indicating particular information, such as employment. To obtain the total number of men working in factories, for example, the data cards were placed one by one over mercury-filled cups. The machine dropped rows of telescoping pins onto the surface of the card. Wherever there was a hole, a pin dropped through the hole into the mercury, thus completing an electrical circuit and activating a switch. The closing switch caused a needle on a dial to jump one or more spaces, depending on the information on the card. When all of the cards were passed through the machine, the desired answer showed directly on the dial.

Hollerith's error detector was a bell. Every time the counter was incremented, the bell rang. A card that did not ring the bell was pulled out for examination.

Instead of a tabulation time in the order of 7.5 years estimated for the manual tabulation of the 1880 census, the 1890 census was tabulated in under two months.

Hollerith then decided to enter the commercial market and

Fig. 8.3. The introduction of Hollerith's system in the 1890 Census. (*Courtesy of IBM*)

in 1896 he organized the Tabulating Machine Company. He owned the machines used in the 1900 census and rented them to the government. Railroads bought Hollerith's machines to audit their freight statistics. Insurance companies classified their risks and merchandising houses kept track of their sales with his machines. As soon as the value of the machine became clear, the

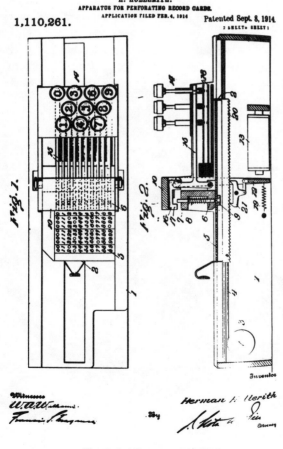

Fig. 8.4. (*Courtesy of IBM*)

Tabulating Machine Company was off and running. (See Figures 8.4, 8.5, and 8.6.)

Hollerith, however, did not get the contract he wanted most—the work of the 1910 census. The bureau had decided to set up its own facilities, later named the Mechanical Laboratory, for developing and making tabulating machinery so that it would not have to depend entirely on Hollerith and pay his high rental fees.

The new director of the bureau, S. N. North, gave the job of devising better tabulating techniques to James Powers, who astutely stipulated that he was to retain the patent rights to any machines he developed. Shortly after the census was made, Powers left the bureau and in 1911 formed the Powers Accounting Machine Company, which became the major supplier of equipment to the bureau.

In 1911, the year in which Powers formed his company, Hollerith's company merged with the International Time Recording Company, the Dayton Scale Company, and the Bundy Manufacturing Corporation to form the Computing-Tabulat-

Fig. 8.5. Hollerith's punch. (*Courtesy of IBM*)

ing-Recording Company (CTR), a holding company. In 1924 CTR was renamed the International Business Machine Corporation, and in 1933, IBM was reorganized and became an operating corporation.

In 1927 the Powers Accounting Machine Company became

Fig. 8.6. Hollerith's tabulator. (*Courtesy of IBM*)

the Tabulating Machines Division of the Remington-Rand Corporation. In 1955 Remington-Rand merged with Sperry Gyroscope to form the Sperry-Rand Corporation. Hollerith and Powers thus started two of the giants of American business.

Hollerith remained as a consultant to IBM until 1921. He died in 1929. IBM is still the custodian of Hollerith's legacy to it, the punched card. From the early 24-column card the IBM card developed into 45 columns. The 45-column card was used by the Census until 1940. By 1925 the first 80-column equipment was developed, almost doubling the card capacity. The punched card is still the basic unit in the IBM accounting method. In 1969 the company announced its System/3 Model 10, which uses a 96-column card.

In the 1970s the punched card is being deposed as king of the computer. Rivals have appeared—key/tape, key/disk, magnetic ink character recognition, optical character recognition. However, even with the inroads of these competitors in computer input and output, it is probable that Hollerith's manila cards with their mysterious holes will never leave the scene.

Hollerith has given his name to the code used on the standard IBM card. It is explained in Chapter 14.

chapter 9

Electromechanical and Electrical Computers

Babbage's difference engine and analytical engine were strictly mechanical—they operated by gears, ratchets, springs, and so forth. Hollerith applied electricity to his card readers, in particular in the sensing device. In adding machines, an electric motor replaced the hand lever, which had initiated and actuated the operational steps.

Switching is an important development in calculators. If you want a simple desk calculator to perform a second operation on an answer it has produced, you must put the answer back in the calculator and initiate the next routine. The modern electric calculator or computer can switch numbers (representing instructions, data, intermediate solutions, or final answers) from one part of the machine to another. It can switch them from one arithmetic or control unit to another; between these units and memory; or between the input or output devices and memory. You can tell an electronic computer everything you want it to do to accomplish a certain batch of work, and leave it to do the whole thing by itself according to its program. Babbage's analytical engine could go through such a routine by following its punched cards. The switching elements incorporated successively in the computer as it developed were electrical switches, relays, electron tubes, and transistors. They can all exist in two states, ON or OFF, and thus act as binary devices.

109

The development of nonelectronic automatic calculators, principally for scientific use, occupied the period from 1925 to 1945. Then the electronic computers took over. The first generation of electronic computers used circuits with vacuum tubes. The second generation used circuits with transistors and crystal diodes. The third generation uses circuits with silicon chips containing circuit elements so tiny they can hardly be seen without a magnifying glass. (See Figure 9.1.)

The first step in the transition from a mechanical to an electrical computer involves replacing at least some of the wheels and levers with electrical circuits. Machines that are partly mechanical and partly electrical are electromechanical. Early devices of this type were not strictly computers because they could not carry out a predetermined series of instructions stored in their memories.

A step toward providing the switching function essential for a truly automatic calculator was taken by J. W. Bryce and his associates in the development of devices and circuitry that would transfer data between registers or from registers to recording devices. These components were utilized in a machine developed by IBM for Columbia University in 1929; in IBM's multiplying machines introduced in 1931; and ultimately in the Mark I computer.

Science and War

Science owes many of its advances to the exigencies of war. World War I saw many new chemical developments, and World War II of course accelerated the development of the computer and the atom bomb.

The problem of projectiles has been of interest in war and peace ever since the experiments of Galileo and Newton. The calculation of missile trajectories is a tedious mathematical task, and it was soon found that the motions of projectiles were more complicated than had been supposed.

Fig. 9.1. Sixteen-bit flatpack used throughout memory and logic areas of Honeywell's Model 8200 computer system contains an integrated circuit that has the equivalent of 110 second-generation components shown in this photo. (*Courtesy of Honeywell Inc.*)

During World War I ballistics calculations were simplified
by assumptions and approximations of doubtful accuracy. At
the time the U. S. Army had two able groups of men working on
ballistic problems, one headed by Forest Ray Moulton and the
other by Oswald Veblen, the son of the sociologist and
economist Thorstein Veblen. In 1932 Veblen and Albert
Einstein were the first professors at the Institute for Advanced
Study in Princeton. Between wars, ballistics research was
continued by the Ordnance Technical Branch and the Ballistics
Laboratory at Aberdeen Proving Ground.

Calculation of Electrical Circuits

Long mathemathical problems occupied not only ballistics
but also a newer branch of science—electricity. Since the late
nineteenth century physicists and engineers had been formu-
lating problems in circuit theory in mathematical terms. One of
these men was Vannevar Bush of MIT. Bush, like Babbage, was
looking for some mechanical means of doing his tedious
calculations, and in 1927 he and two colleagues produced an
analog device that could solve a variety of problems in electrical
circuits. Its basis was a form of the watt-hour meter that
measures power consumption in the home. It could solve a
first-order equation.

In 1931 Bush described a machine called a differential
analyzer. It was not based on the watt-hour meter, but was
entirely mechanical. Input and output were in the form of
mechanical rotations. The new device intrigued two groups—the
Ballistics Research Laboratory at Aberdeen, and the Moore
School of Electrical Engineering at the University of Pennsylvania. Both groups approached Bush, and in 1933 the Ordnance
Department, the Moore School, and MIT got together on a
design program. Machines were built at Aberdeen and at
Moore.

Bush and others saw that a device to analyze electrical networks experimentally would be a great improvement over long and perhaps impracticable mathematical calculations, and the MIT Network Analyzer was designed.

In 1942 Bush and a colleague built a faster differential analyzer that could be programmed by prepunched paper tape instead of physical interconnections and where information was stored and transmitted by electrical connections instead of shafts.

In 1937 Dr. George Stibitz of Bell Labs wired together some telephone relays and other circuitry to make a kind of digital computer to speed up his calculations. His electromechanical device converted decimal numbers to binary. Stibitz pointed out to his colleagues that he had the basis for an adder to handle any number of binary digits, and that a relay device could do the work of a desk calculator. Stibitz's Complex Number Computer was the first program-controlled electrical digital calculator. It could do a nine-digit division in 30 to 40 seconds and had an error-detecting code.

In 1940 Stibitz demonstrated his computer by remote control before the Mathematical Society of Dartmouth College. According to Stibitz, it was here that Norbert Wiener and Mauchly were introduced to the digital computer.

Meanwhile Claude W. Shannon, also of Bell Labs, had published "A Symbolic Analysis of Relay and Switching Circuits." He drew a parallel between switching circuits and the algebra of logic; true or false values were analogous to open and closed states in electrical circuits. (His ideas are explained more fully in Chapter 5.)

With the advent of World War II Bell Labs developed the Relay Interpolator, which consisted of some 500 telephone relays plus teletype equipment for input, output, and control. The larger ballistic computer followed, then an all-purpose computer with over 9,000 relays, 50 teletype units, and a weight of about 10 tons.

Howard Aiken, Thomas Watson, and the Mark I

The next milestone in electromechanical calculation was the ASCC, or Mark I. It was the joint project of Howard Aiken, professor of applied mathematics at Harvard, and Thomas J. Watson, president of IBM.

Watson was not a designer of machines—he was a salesman and executive—but he had the insight to see the value of Aiken's ideas and to do for him what the chancellor of the exchequer was not willing to do for Babbage—underwrite his invention so that it could become a reality. Watson was the guiding spirit of IBM's great growth; he was president until 1952, when his son took over the title, and chief executive officer until shortly before his death in 1956. (See Figure 9.2.)

Thomas J. Watson's motto was THINK, and he made a lot of people, in particular his competitors, think long and hard. Actually he was more inclined to get out and hustle than to sit and think.

In 1892 Watson took a job as bookkeeper in a butcher shop in Elmira, New York. Like our other geniuses, he found manual bookkeeping painful. He gave it up for a congenial job—selling pianos, organs, and sewing machines. He liked being a one-man operation—manager, accountant, and deliveryman all in one. In 1894 he moved to Buffalo and eventually became a salesman for the National Cash Register Company.

The NCR had a problem: other companies were reconditioning and selling used NCR machines, which were in competition with new cash registers. John H. Patterson, NCR's president, decided to organize a secret subsidiary to take over the used cash register business.

Patterson picked Watson out of 400 salesmen to head his new subsidiary. Watson was given a million dollars to spend without having to account for its allocation. He proved to be an able guerrilla fighter; he opened up stores near those of the competition, undersold them, and lured away their salesmen.

Fig. 9.2. Thomas J. Watson. (*Courtesy of IBM*)

The competition was soon as dead as a doornail, and at age 33 Watson was the third man at NCR. At first Watson was Patterson's favorite, but like Lucifer, he aspired too high and aroused Patterson's jealousy. He was fired.

Watson then took a job as manager of Hollerith's ailing

Computing-Tabulating-Recording Company (CTR). In three months he was president. He shortly negotiated an agreement with a major competitor, the Powers Accounting Machine Company. In six years CTR's gross income went from $4 million to almost $14 million. In the recession of 1921, however, annual sales fell to $3.5 million. With the astute backing of Alexander H. Hemphill, president of the Guaranty Trust Company, Watson expanded the business beyond just tabulating machines, and times got better. In his decade with the company Watson had sparked the development of better equipment—a tabulating printer, an efficient keypunch, a horizontal sorter. In 1924 the name of the company was changed to International Business Machines.

Watson was a man of violent temper and iron whim who would promote or fire a man on impulse.

The depression of the thirties slowed Watson little. Instead of curtailing production and the payroll, he kept on building up a huge surplus inventory. It was a gamble that paid off. Soon IBM got the contract to process the data for the Social Security System when it was established in 1935, and World War II brought a new flood of government business. Watson was also responsible for building IBM's matchless sales organization.

Watson became a public figure, the first of a new breed, the socially conscious industrialist, and he tried to put Roosevelt's New Deal across to businessmen. As a lifelong Democrat, he could have been an ambassador, but chose to become a kind of unofficial ambassador in international circles—to the incidental benefit of IBM.

Even in the midst of furious production, Watson also had an eye for the future—which brings us back to his underwriting of Howard Aiken's project.

In 1937 Aiken, a graduate student at Harvard, was trying to make a computer to solve certain mathematical problems. He had concluded that a computer was a computer—that all digital machines used the same basic logic, and that a general-purpose computer could be built that could handle not only his special mathematical problems but any kind of problem.

Aiken's proposal for such a machine came to the attention of the Watson Computing Bureau at Columbia, and they and Watson bought his ideas. Watson let Aiken write his own ticket and gave him four top IBM engineers as helpers. Work started in 1939.

The work took five years. In 1944 the Automatic Sequence Controlled Calculator, or Mark I, was formally presented to Harvard University by Watson. (See Figure 9.3.) As Aiken noted, it was Babbage's dream come true. The calculator used advances in mechanical and electrical engineering to realize Babbage's ideas and to go beyond them.

Fig. 9.3. The Automatic Sequence Controlled Calculator—Mark I. (*Courtesy of IBM*)

The new machine consisted largely of standard Hollerith counters with a superimposed and specially designed automatic tape sequence control for directing the operations of the machine. The ASCC was an electromechanical device 51 feet long and 8 feet high; it had more than 760,000 parts, including 500 miles of wire. It was a parallel synchronous calculator, using a number length of 23 decimal digits plus algebraic signs (it could also use 46 digits). The machine could carry out any specified sequence of five fundamental operations—addition, subtraction, multiplication, division, and reference to tables of results already computed.

The Mark I had 60 registers for constants, 72 adding storage registers, a central multiplying and dividing unit, means of computing the elementary transcendental functions $\log_{10}x$, 10^x and $\sin x$, and three interpolators reading functions coded in perforated paper tapes. The input was in the form of punched cards and switch positions. The output was punched into cards or printed by electric typewriters.

Each of the 60 constant registers consisted of 24 ten-position switches (for the 23 digits and the sign). Each of the 72 adding storage registers was composed of 24 electromechanical counter wheels for adding and storing numbers. Each of these was essentially a ten-position switch (with additional contacts for carries) actuated through a magnetic clutch. Subtraction was done by the same counter wheels by complementary numbers. The multiply-divide unit multiplied by first forming and storing the nine integer multiples of the multiplicand; then selecting the multiples indicated by each digit of the multiplier and shifting and adding them in the proper columnar position. The position of the decimal point was fixed and determined by a plugboard. Division was carried out with the same unit in much the same way: the nine integer multiples of the divisor were first formed and stored. These multiples were then compared with the dividend, and the largest multiple smaller than the dividend was selected; it was subtracted from the dividend, and a digit defining it was entered in the quotient register.

Logarithms, antilogarithms, and sines were calculated automatically by means of special registers and appropriate series expansions of the functions. Each of the three interpolators carried an endless function tape containing values of the function of equidistant arguments, together with appropriate interpolation coefficients. The tape was first positioned by moving it automatically in the direction of shortest travel; then the function was read by the machine and the interpolated value was calculated.

The sequence mechanism consisted of a sprocket drum over which ran a perforated paper tape, the "control" tape. Each transverse line of the tape had space for 24 equidistant holes in three groups, A, B, and C, of 8 holes each. Each line of holes constituted the instruction: "Take the number out of unit A, deliver it to B, start operation C." The sequence and interpolator mechanisms and the counter wheels were all synchronized and driven by a gear-connected mechanical system and a 5-hp motor. The fundamental cycle was 300 milliseconds. A typical multiplication took about 3 seconds.

The Mark I as originally built could make limited decisions by making comparisons. For example, it could be instructed to compare A to B, and if they were equal, to follow a certain course of action, but it they were not equal, to follow another course. In 1943, while the first general-purpose electromechanical computer was being built, work was started on the ENIAC, the first electronic computer.

The Mark II was constructed by the Harvard Laboratory under Aiken's direction. It was unveiled in 1947, and was subsequently turned over to the Dahlgren Proving Ground to solve problems in the ballistics of guided missiles and supersonic aerodynamics for the U. S. Navy.

The Mark II was three times as large as the Mark I and 12

times as fast. It was a relay, or all-electrical, calculator in comparison with the electromechanical design of the Mark I. Input was by punched paper tape and output was by teletype. Plug-in parts made it possible to replace faulty components without disturbing other sections of the machine. For simpler mathematical work the machine could be separated into two parts to do separate calculations at the same time. Errors were signaled by a complex alarm and light system. Aesthetically the Mark II was "a sprawling structure of panels, wiring, switchboards, and electrical circuits." The unveiling of the Mark II was part of the program of the first general scientific meeting on large-scale digital calculating machines. The four-day symposium attracted 250 experts.

chapter 10

From ENIAC to UNIVAC

The electromechanical computer and the electrical computer were great devices, but their days were short because the electronic computer was waiting in the wings. It offered an improvement in speed of more than 500 to 1.

The first machine to use vacuum tubes for digital computation was designed by John V. Atanasoff, a professor at Iowa State who studied Bush's analyzer. In 1940, with a colleague, he built a prototype device to solve simultaneous linear equations. Data was to be stored on capacitors and punch cards. Although the machine was never perfected for service, it caught the interest of John W. Mauchly, who met Atanasoff in 1941, around the time Mauchly came to the Moore School of the University of Pennsylvania, already a computational center. At that time another computational center, the Ballistics Research Laboratory, was frantically trying to meet the demands of the war effort.

World War II found the United States entirely unprepared for combat. In 1939 the regular army consisted of some 120,000 officers and men. Its scientific and logistic support was supplied by the Ordnance Department, which was staffed by a handful of officers and career civilians. Its only scientific facility was the Aberdeen Proving Ground, which rose heroically to the occasion. One of its important functions was the production of firing and bombing tables and related gun control data. The computing group at Aberdeen was composed of highly skilled civilians. They used desk calculators and the Bush differential analyzer; the latter was subject to breakdowns, but it was all they had. There was a larger version of the Bush machine at the Moore School, and the Ordnance Department contracted for its use. The Moore engineers developed an electronic torque amplifier to replace the mechanical ones on the Bush machines and thus eliminated the principal cause of the breakdowns.

Meantime Lieutenant Herman Goldstine, a Ph.D. in mathematics stationed at Aberdeen, was assigned to the University of Pennsylvania to supervise the computational and training work going on there.

In the group at the Moore School were two men greatly interested in the problems of computation and computers —John W. Mauchly and J. Presper Eckert.

Mauchly got a Ph.D. in physics from Johns Hopkins in 1932. He taught physics in several colleges, and analyzed geophysical data for the Carnegie Institution, where he was snowed under by the volume of calculations and became interested in the idea of designing a highly sophisticated electronic calculator. He had already invented a special kind of digital computer that used neon or gas tubes for storage, and tried using a teletype terminal for handling masses of data, which he thought might be speeded up with vacuum tubes. A man Mauchly scarcely knew kept urging him to keep on experimenting because computers had a great potential. The man was Norbert Wiener.

Mauchly came to the Moore School when he was 34, attracted by the opportunity to study its differential analyzer. Here he met J. Presper Eckert, then 22, an instructor.

Eckert had many interests, among them a device for measuring the strength of very small magnetic fields, which might detect mines and submarines. He also worked with radar.

Eckert got his M.A. in 1943 and accepted an invitation to work with Mauchly on the serious problem of calculating gun trajectories. Electromechanical devices could calculate some 50 times faster than a man with a desk calculator, but this still wasn't good enough. A typical firing table called for several thousand trajectories, and the war might be over before they could be compiled at the current rate. The relay computers were controlled electrically, but it took time for the relays to open and close, and it was this time that must be cut down.

Up until that time analog devices had proved to be faster than digital devices such as Babbage's calculators. But digital devices offered advantages in accuracy, adaptability, and number of decimal places to be attained. The marriage of the digital computer with the vacuum tube seemed the best bet.

In 1942, at the request of army men at the Moore School, Mauchly and Eckert submitted an informal memo on the construction of an electronic computer that could calculate firing tables. The memo lay buried for almost a year until Goldstine heard of it and had it reconstructed from notes. He submitted it in Washington, and the Ordnance Department authorized a development program at the Moore School. Work on the machine was given the go-ahead on April 9, 1943, by Colonel Leslie E. Simon at the urging of Prof. Oswald Veblen of the Institute for Advanced Study. Veblen listened briefly to Goldstine's presentation and said, "Give him the money."

The project was supervised by Prof. Brainerd of the University of Pennsylvania, and Goldstine was the supervisor for the government and also contributed original mathematical work. Mauchly and Eckert were the geniuses of the effort. Mauchly was the innovator, the idea man; Eckert, as chief engineer, established standards for components, including their failure rate, and largely debugged the machine before it was built.

The new dream calculator was named the Electronic Numerical Integrator and Computer, or ENIAC. At that time not too much was known about vacuum tubes, in particular their reliability. To avoid breakdowns, tubes were operated at less than rated voltage and never turned off. All tubes were operated as on-off binary devices, not as analog devices in which the magnitude of the output represents a number. Tubes were utilized in a minimum of basic circuit combinations to simplify the design. Circuits were constructed from rigidly tested standard components, which were operated at levels below their normal ratings. With these precautions the ENIAC proved to be as reliable as the electromechanical machines in rate of failure with time and enormously more reliable in rate of failure with number of calculations.

The ENIAC was placed in operation at the Moore School, component by component, beginning with the cycling unit and an accumulator. Final assembly was done in the fall of 1945.

The ENIAC was a monster. (See Figure 10.1.) It had 30 separate units (plus power supply and forced-air cooling), occupied a space 30 by 50 feet, and weighed over 30 tons. It had some 18,000 vacuum tubes, 70,000 resistors, 10,000 capacitors, and 6,000 switches. It was a synchronous machine with a clock rate of 100,000 pulses per second. The ENIAC had 20 accumulators (for addition and subtraction), a multiplier, and a combination divider and square rooter. Input and output were by punched cards. Tables could be automatically printed from the cards by an IBM tabulator. Each accumulator contained 10 ring counters of 10 stages each and a two-stage ring counter for the sign. Carry circuits were provided. Subtraction was by complements.

The ENIAC was the prototype of most modern computers. It embodied almost all the components and concepts that became standard in later machines. Its designers developed such standard elements as the gate (logical AND element), buffer (logical OR element), and flip-flop (logical high-speed device for storage and control). The machine's counters and accumulators were made up of combinations of these basic elements.

Fig. 10.1. The ENIAC. (*Courtesy of UNIVAC*)

The machine could discriminate the sign of a number, compare quantitites for equality, add, subtract, multiply, divide, and extract square roots. It stored up to 20 .10-digit decimal numbers. Its accumulators combined the functions of an adding machine and storage unit. There was no central memory as such; storage was localized within the functioning units of the computer.

The gate, or switch, consisted of a single pentode with a control voltage applied to its suppressor grid. Its function was similar to that of a single-pole switch in that it "opened" (passed a pulse pattern) when the suppressor grid was positive and "closed" when the grid was negative.

The buffer had two or more tubes connected through a common load resistor to form a circuit with the logical properties of the word OR. The grids of the tubes were normally biased at the cutoff point so that a positive input to any tube in the combination produced a negative output.

The flip-flop circuit contained two triodes connected so that only one would conduct at any given time. This bistable device had two inputs and two outputs. In the normal, or set, position, one side of the output was positive, the other negative. In the abnormal, or reset, position, these polarities were reversed. A group of ten flip-flops (0–9), interconnected to count digit pulses, formed a decade ring counter for adding and storing numbers. Ten decade ring counters, one per decimal place, plus one PM (sign) counter, formed the basic arithmetic and storage unit of the ENIAC—the accumulator. The decade ring counters had ten transmission circuits so that when any ring passed the nine positions, a pulse was passed to the next ring in the series. Input pulses reaching the accumulator added to or subtracted from its contents.

The accumulator was used in all arithmetic operations. Two were used in addition, the contents of one being transferred to the other; and two in subtraction, done by a complement-and-add process. In multiplication, four accumulators stored the multiplier and multiplicand and accumulated the partial products. In division, they shifted the remainder and stored the numerator, denominator, and quotient. Accumulators were used by the function table to store the argument and accumulate the function value. The main purpose of the function tables, which actually were banks of resistor matrices controlled by switches, was to store the arbitrary functions called for by the problem. The switches selected one of 12 digits and two signs for each of the 104 values of an independent variable that were stored in each table.

Addition required 20 pulse times (0.2 millisecond); multiplication, 14 addition times (2.8 milliseconds).

These operations required that the background wiring of

the machine be prepared. Plugged connections and switches instituted the cycling of addition, etc., under control of the cycling unit. Setting up these connections for new problems might require from a half-hour to a whole day, and limited the flexibility of the system. The limitation was not serious in the production of firing tables, but in the late 1940s a more flexible wired programming system was devised from suggestions made by John von Neumann. The background wiring was fixed and the function tables were utilized to store instructions rather than the values of functions. These instructions did not actually constitute an internally stored program since they had to be set manually on the function-table switches.

The ENIAC was formally dedicated in 1946. During 1946 it remained at the Moore School, doing problems in ballistics and atomic energy. Then it was dismantled and moved to Aberdeen and debugged, and its true worth became apparent. It had taken a skilled operator about 20 hours to compute a 60-second trajectory, and had taken the differential analyzer 15 minutes. The ENIAC did it in 30 seconds—half the time it took the projectile to reach its target.

The ENIAC was out front in the computer field through 1952. However, newer computers were more economical than the ENIAC, and on October 2, 1955, its power was disconnected. Sections of it are preserved in various museums. (See Figure 10.2.)

Von Neumann and the EDVAC and IAS

While the ENIAC was still in the construction stage, a better machine, the EDVAC, was in an advanced stage of design. It was to have fewer tubes, larger and cheaper storage, a shorter setup time, and the ability to handle more types of problems.

Meantime the Moore School had acquired another dis-

Fig. 10.2. Mauchly (center) and Eckert (right) at "Computer in the Park." Chicago Museum of Science, 1971. (*Courtesy of UNIVAC*)

tinguished consultant in John von Neumann. He was born in Budapest, and was a linguist as well as a scientist, with the uncanny faculty of total recall. He had a degree in chemical engineering, and earned his Ph.D. in mathematics when he was 22. In 1933 he went to the Institute for Advanced Study at Princeton. Von Neumann's principal interest was the application of mathematics. He studied the problems of supersonic and turbulent fluid flow, and in World War II was an expert on shock and detonation waves for Aberdeen, the Manhattan Project, and other government agencies.

In 1944 Goldstine took von Neumann to see the ENIAC, and von Neumann was at once hooked on computers. He began developing Eckert's suggestion of a delay line for storing information in a computer.

The ultrasonic delay line transforms an electrical signal into an ultrasonic signal in some fluid and then transforms it back to an electrical signal. The signal is delayed because it travels much more slowly through a fluid than through a wire. The delay time is set by adjusting the length of the container of fluid. If the input and output of the delay line are connected, the signals keep circulating in the line, which may be tapped to enter or retrieve signals. Shockley at MIT built the first delay line, and Eckert and others at the Moore School built the second in 1943. Piezoelectric crystals transformed the electrical signal to a sonic signal and vice versa.

In the ENIAC a binary digit required a flip-flop, or pair of vacuum tubes, to store a binary digit. In the delay line 1,000 binary digits could be stored at no more than the cost of 10 vacuum tubes. The delay line stored both numbers and instructions. One of von Neumann's many contributions to the EDVAC was the stored program. He devised a sorting and merging program—the first stored program to be written. He was also responsible for doing away with parallel operations (implemented on the ENIAC by 20 accumulators) and doing one operation at a time. His argument was that the computer is so fast that serial operation is adequate, and it is simpler and cheaper. However, this philosophy was reversed in later machines because in the serial machine the control is much more complex.

The EDVAC (Electronic Discrete Variable Automatic Computer) was built at the Moore School between 1947 and 1950, destined for Aberdeen. It was a serial, synchronous machine. It contained some 5,900 vacuum tubes and about 12,000 semiconductor diodes, and used a word length of 44 binary digits.

The internal memory was composed of 128 thermostatically controlled acoustic delay lines, each storing 384 bits (and accommodating 8 words) as sound waves in mercury; the information circulated constantly through the line. Thus 1,024 (128 × 8) words of fast-access storage were available, with an access time of 48 to 384 microseconds.

The EDVAC had diode logic circuits. Subtraction was done directly, not through complements. Average time for addition was 864 microseconds and for multiplication, 2,900 microseconds. Input/output media included paper tape, teletypewriters, and punched cards.

Important features of the EDVAC were used subsequently in the UNIVAC and in other machines.

Von Neumann was a philosopher and a highly articulate writer as well as a mathematician. His famous paper, "The General and Logical Theory of Automata," compared the operation of living organisms with the operation of machines.

The EDVAC was accepted in 1950 and moved to Aberdeen. The Moore School had lost interest in computers and made no effort to retain Eckert, Mauchly, von Neumann, and the rest of the ENIAC-EDVAC staff. Von Neumann returned to the Institute for Advanced Study at Princeton, where Goldstine joined him. In 1946 Eckert and Mauchly departed to form their own company, the Electronic Control Company.

Goldstine and von Neumann continued their work on the development of computers. A project was finally undertaken at the Institute, sponsored by the Institute, various government departments, Princeton University, and RCA. The IAS computer was developed in 1946–1952 under von Neumann's direction. It was an electronic parallel asynchronous fixed-point machine. It was only 2 by 8 feet (exclusive of input/output equipment). It contained some 2,300 vacuum tubes (mostly double triodes) and consisted essentially of three registers, a vacuum-tube parallel adder, a control unit, and an electrostatic memory composed of 40 CRTs. A magnetic drum was added later. Input/output consisted of punched cards and teletype tape. The electostatic memory had a capacity of 1,024 40-bit words and consisted of an array of $32 \times 32 = 1,024$ charged spots on the phosphor surface of each cathode-ray tube. The storage tube was faster than the ultrasonic delay line.

Negative numbers were represented by complements. Multiplication was done by successive addition and division by successive subtraction. The IAS was a stored-program machine with the instruction stored in the CRT memory. The basic "machine language" or set of instructions included commands for the basic arithmetic operations, shifting, input, output, unconditional transfer, and conditional transfer (branching). The IAS machine established the general structure of the modern computer.

The computer revolution was now gathering momentum throughout the United States and western Europe. Before the IAS computer was finished, one of its designers left to head a group at the Rand Corporation in Santa Monica. He and his co-workers built the JOHNNIAC (it was named for John von Neumann, but von Neumann did not like the name). It was accepted in March 1954. The Atomic Energy Commission's laboratories built copies of it.

Later on Goldstine became director of mathematical research at the IBM Research Center.

The UNIVAC I

In 1946 Eckert and Mauchly's new company started the design of the BINAC, or Binary Automatic Computer, a mercury delay line machine. It was the first American machine built after the ENIAC and became operational in August 1950. (See Figure 10.3.) The BINAC was cheaper and faster than the ENIAC and EDVAC and could handle magnetic tapes instead of punched cards. Two BINACs were built, together comprising a single system. However, each machine could operate independently.

Eckert and Mauchly were short of capital for their new

Fig. 10.3. The BINAC. (*Courtesy of UNIVAC*)

company, and the Munn brothers, owners of the Totalizator Company, bought an interest in the business. In 1949 the Munns went to their friend Jim Rand for advice about their new investment.

James H. Rand, Jr. was a shrewd and hard-driving entrepreneur. With his father he had formed the Rand Kardex Corporation, and by 1927 his company had combined with the Remington Typewriter Company and numerous other companies to form Remington Rand. By 1951 the company had completed an electronic model of the Powers tabulating machine. At that time most computers were built to handle complex scientific problems. Rand saw that computers could also be enormously useful in business.

Fig. 10.4. Mercury Memory Prototype Test Unit for UNIVAC I. (*Courtesy of UNIVAC*)

Rand bought the Eckert-Mauchly company in 1950 and made Eckert vice-president of his computer division. He had the money to back the venture—millions were put into it before a single computer was sold. Mauchly and Eckert had already largely developed what was to become the UNIVAC I (Universal Automatic Computer). It became the first commercially feasible computer that was self-checking and able to handle both numbers and descriptive data.

The UNIVAC I was a serial, synchronous machine. It contained some 5,000 vacuum tubes and several times as many semiconductor diodes in logic and clamp circuits. One hundred mercury delay lines provided 1,000 words of 12 decimal digits for internal storage. (See Figure 10.4.) Twelve additional delay lines were used as input/output registers. Except for console switches and an electric typewriter that provided small items of information, the input/output medium was metal-base magnetic tape. A line printer was added several years later.

Programs were stored. Through the use of a six-bit code, alphabetic characters, punctuation, control symbols, etc. could be handled by the machine as well as decimal digits.

There were some 45 distinct instructions. Addition took 0.5 millisecond and multiplication about 2.5 milliseconds.

Soon after the UNIVAC I was put into operation, "automatic programming" techniques were developed for it by its designers. These techniques have evolved into extensive programming languages.

The first UNIVAC I system was delivered to the Bureau of the Census in 1951. It was used almost continuously around the clock for over 12 years. In 1963 it was retired after more than 73,000 hours of operation. Some of it is in the Smithsonian Institution. In all, 48 UNIVAC I machines were built.

In 1955 Remington Rand merged with Sperry Gyroscope Corporation, founded in 1910. J. Presper Eckert stayed with UNIVAC and is now a vice-president. John Mauchly eventually formed his own consulting business.

chapter 11

Alan M. Turing

Alan Mathison Turing, born in 1912, was an English mathematical genius who contributed much to the theory of automata. From his early days at school Turing cared only about science and mathematics. He liked to work everything out from first principles—witness his later Turing machine—and was given to experiments not too popular at his school: his housemaster mentions "heaven knows what witches' brew blazing on a naked wooden window sill."

He went to King's College, Cambridge, in 1931. In 1935 he began work in mathematical logic and started on his best-known investigation, on computable numbers and the Turing machine. His published results attracted attention and led to his spending 1936–1938 in Princeton. Shortly after he returned to Cambridge the war broke out and he spent the next six years with the Foreign Office, aborting his scientific work at a time when he probably would have been highly productive. He received the OBE for his government service.

After the war he turned to the new automatic computing machines, which were in principle realizations of his "universal machine" described in a 1937 paper. He joined a group at the National Physical Laboratory which was to design and construct a large computer, eventually named the ACE. He liked the diversity of the work, which ranged from electrical circuit design

135

to the entirely new field of organizing mathematical problems for a machine.

In some respects ACE improved on the ENIAC. It was a binary machine that used punched cards and a mercury delay-line memory. The ACE had no rival in England for the next five years. Turing also worked on the Manchester Automatic Digital Machine (MADAM), said to have more memory capacity than any other computer of its day.

Turing was a charming man, with the enthusiasm of a child for his new ideas, serious or fanciful. He was devoted to his friends. For recreation he amused himself with his home-made experiments, often Rube Goldberg devices. He died in 1954.

Turing's work had a central theme: the extent and the limitations of mechanistic explanations of nature. His ideas meshed with Norbert Wiener's concept of cybernetics, which Wiener defined as the science of control and communications in the animal and the machine.

The Turing machine is the theoretical bare bones of a computer; it is not a practical device. It consists of a tape, divided into squares the width of the tape; some kind of a scanner to read what is written on the tape; a device for writing and erasing X's and 1's; a dial with numbers and a pointer; and a control or instruction device.

The machine can do only these things: write an X or a 1 in a blank square; erase an X or a 1; move the tape one square forward or backward; emit a signal and stop when it has finished its work. In the simplest model, the control unit consists merely of a table in which the next instruction can be looked up. The reading and writing unit can consist simply of somebody with a pencil and an eraser. The tables can give instructions for addition, multiplication, exponentiation, etc. In effect, an instruction will tell the operator: If the dial is set at 4, and the square being scanned contains a 1, erase the 1 and set the dial at 2. This primitive computer used the written symbols for input and output, and the dial for the memory unit.

Turing believed that a machine of this kind could be made to do any piece of work which could be done by a human computer obeying explicit instructions given to him before the work starts. Such a machine is completely specified by a table, which states how it moves from each of the finite sets of possible configurations to another.

The machine we described was supplied with a blank tape. But we may also imagine a machine supplied with a tape already bearing a pattern that will influence its subsequent operation, and this pattern might be the table, suitably encoded, of a particular computing machine, X. It could be arranged that this tape would cause the machine, M, into which it was inserted to behave like machine X.

Turing proved the fundamental result that there is a "universal machine," U (of which he gave the table), which can be made to do the work of any assigned special-purpose machine, that is to say, to carry out any piece of computing, if a tape bearing suitable instructions is inserted into it. Turing's paper "Can a Machine Think?" is a classic.

We quote some paragraphs.

This special property of digital computers, that they can mimic any discrete state machine, is described by saying that they are *universal* machines. The existence of machines with this property has the important consequence that, considerations of speed apart, it is unneccesary to design various new machines to do various computing processes. They can all be done with one digital computer, suitably programmed for each case. It will be seen that as a consequence of this all digital computers are in a sense equivalent.

The original question, "Can machines think?" I believe to be too meaningless to deserve discussion. Nevertheless I believe that at the end of the century the use of words and general educated opinion will have altered so much that one will be able to speak of machines thinking without expecting to be contradicted. I believe further that no useful purpose is served by concealing these beliefs. The popular view that scientists proceed inexorably from well-established fact to well-established fact, never being influenced by any unproved conjecture, is quite mistaken. Provided it is made clear which are proved facts and which are conjectures, no harm can result. Conjectures are of great importance since they suggest useful lines of research.

I now proceed to consider opinions opposed to my own.

(1) *The Theological Objection.* Thinking is a function of man's immortal soul. God has given an immortal soul to every man and woman, but not to any other animal or to machines. Hence no animal or machine can think.

I am unable to accept any part of this, but will attempt to reply in theological terms. I should find the argument more convincing if animals were classed with men, for there is a greater difference, to my mind, between the typical animate and the inanimate than there is between man and the other animals. The arbitrary character of the orthodox view becomes clearer if we consider how it might appear to a member of some other religious community. How do Christians regard the Moslem view that women have no souls? ...

However, this is mere speculation. I am not very impressed with theological arguments whatever they may be used to support. Such arguments have often been found unsatisfactory in the past. In the time of Galileo it was argued that the texts, "And the sun stood still ... and hasted not to go down about a whole day" (Joshua x. 13) and "He laid the foundations of the earth, that it should not move at any time" (Psalm cv. 5) were an adequate refutation of the Copernican theory. With our present knowledge such an argument appears futile. When that knowledge was not available it made a quite different impression.

(2) *The "Heads in the Sand" Objection.* "The consequences of machines thinking would be too dreadful. Let us hope and believe that they cannot do so."

This argument is seldom expressed quite so openly as in the form above. But it affects most of us who think about it at all. We like to believe that Man is in some subtle way superior to the rest of creation. It is best if he can be shown to be *necessarily* superior, for then there is no danger of him losing his commanding position. The popularity of the theological argument is clearly connected with this feeling. It is likely to be quite strong in intellectual people, since they value the power of thinking more highly than others, and are more inclined to base their belief in the superiority of Man on this power.

I do not think that this argument is sufficiently substantial to require refutation. Consolation would be more appropriate: perhaps this should be sought in the transmigration of souls.

(3) *The Mathematical Objection.* There are a number of results of mathematical logic which can be used to show that there are limitations to the powers of discrete-state machines.

The short answer to this argument is that although it is established that there are limitations to the powers of any particular machine, it has only been stated, without any sort of proof, that no such limitations apply to the human intellect. But I do not think this view can be dismissed quite so lightly. ...

(4) *The Argument from Consciousness.* This argument is very well expressed in *Professor Jefferson's* Lister Oration for 1949, from which I quote. "Not until a machine can write a sonnet or compose a concerto because of thoughts and emotions felt, and not by the chance fall of symbols, could we agree that machine equals brain—that is, not only write it but know that it had written it. No mechanism could feel (and not merely artifically signal, an easy contrivance) pleasure at its successes, grief when its valves fuse, be warmed by flattery, be made miserable by its mistakes, be charmed by sex, be angry or depressed when it cannot get what it wants." ...

I am sure that Professor Jefferson does not wish to adopt the extreme and solipsist point of view. Probably he would be quite willing to accept the imitation game as a test. The game (with the player B omitted) is frequently used in practice under the name of *viva voce* to discover whether some one really understands something or has "learnt it parrot fashion." Let us listen in to a part of such a *viva voce*:

Interrogator: In the first line of your sonnet which reads "Shall I compare thee to a summer's day," would not "a spring day" do as well or better?

Witness: It wouldn't scan.

Interrogator: How about "a winter's day." That would scan all right.

Witness: Yes, but nobody wants to be compared to a winter's day.

Interrogator: Would you say Mr. Pickwick reminded you of Christmas?

Witness: In a way.

Interrogator: Yet Christmas is a winter's day, and I do not think Mr. Pickwick would mind the comparison.

Witness: I don't think you're serious. By a winter's day one means a typical winter's day, rather than a special one like Christmas.

And so on. What would Professor Jefferson say if the sonnet-writing machine was able to answer like this in the *viva voce*? ...

I do not wish to give the impression that I think there is no mystery about consciousness. There is, for instance, something of a paradox connected with any attempt to localise it. But I do not think these mysteries necessarily need to be solved before we can answer the question with which we are concerned in this paper.

(5) *Arguments from Various Disabilities.* These arguments take the form, "I grant you that you can make machines do all the things you have mentioned but you will never be able to make one to do X." Numerous features X are suggested in this connexion.

The criticism that a machine cannot have much diversity of behavior is just a way of saying that it cannot have much storage capacity. Until fairly recently a storage capacity of even a thousand digits was very rare.

chapter 12

Memory Elements in a Computer

The Semiconductor

Babbage's mechanical calculator was displaced by the electro-mechanical and then the electrical computer, and these were in turn nudged out by the electronic computer. The 18,000 tubes of the ENIAC no longer glow; they have been darkened by a mighty mite called a transistor.

The Bell Telephone Laboratories evolved the transistor after many years of study on the properties of semiconductors. The inventors of the transistor, John Bardeen, Walter H. Brattain, and William B. Shockley, received the Nobel Prize for physics in 1956. The transistor was soon seen to have an advantage over the electron tube because it was smaller, consumed less power, had a longer life, and was sturdier and more reliable.

The emitter and base of the transistor correspond to the cathode and anode of an electron tube. As in the vacuum tube, a signal between the emitter and the base controls the flow of current, which becomes an amplified picture of the control signal.

Semiconductors can conduct electricity by either or both of two kinds of carriers of electrical charge. One kind, the conduction electron, has a negative charge. The other kind is called a hole because it is a shortage of one electron in the valence bond structure. This deficiency (a positive charge) may be filled by an electron from another valence bond, leaving another hole behind it, so that the hole moves through the crystal. Controlled impurities in the crystal cause either electrons or holes to predominate, and the semiconductor to become N-type or P-type.

The transistor serves as a switch, and small transistors serve as elements of memory units. A transistorized memory unit can store a binary digit with a very small power consumption. Transistors also lend themselves to use in integrated circuits, which are fabricated as entire circuits instead of as individual elements. A silicon chip some 1.5 mm in size can contain a number of such interconnected elements. Fabrication techniques are automatic. The transistor and particularly the integrated circuit have greatly reduced the size and cost of the computer. The transistor also has a number of properties that make it useful as a sensor of light, magnetism, and nuclear radiation. It can produce a laser beam.

Magnetic Core

The most common type of main storage is magnetic core. (See Figure 12.1.) It usually consists of hundreds of thousands of tiny ferrite rings, or cores, a few hundredths of an inch in diameter. Wires pass through the cores so that they can be magnetized, with a polarity depending on the direction of the current. Magnetism in one direction represents a 1 and in the other direction a 0; thus each core represents a binary digit. The cores are organized in grids or planes so that only one core in each plane can be sensed (that is, read from or written to) at a time. Cores came into use around 1950.

Magnetic core is fast and compact, but it is expensive.

Computer systems usually contain cheaper types of on-line storage also when there are large quantities of data to be processed and fast access to all the data and programs is not necessary. Some extra storages transfer data to main storage for processing and some are used directly.

Magnetic Drums

The magnetic drum, once used as main storage, is now usually relegated to auxiliary storage. Its contents must be transferred to main storage for processing. A magnetized area on the metallic-coated steel drum surface represents a 1, and an unmagnetized area represents a 0. A stationary read/write head senses each channel on the rotating drum when the data arrives at the proper position. Instead of a metal surface, some drums are plated with a nickel-cobalt alloy; others are wrapped with a magnetizable metal wire; still others are sprayed with a ferrite "paint" similar to the coating on magnetic tape.

Magnetic Disks

This storage consists of a stack of thin metal disks mounted on a vertical shaft. Read/write heads on movable access arms sense the data, recorded as magnetic spots on the concentric tracks of the rotating disks. Each side of a disk may have 500 of these grooveless tracks, and a file might have 25 disks for a total capacity of over a million bytes. Head-per-track disks have stationary read/write heads for each track of each disk, and are much faster than the movable-head disks. Disk drives come with removable and replaceable packs.

Fig. 12.1. Magnetic cores. (*Courtesy of IBM*)

Magnetic Tape

Magnetic tape is a popular means of storage and in-put/output. The plastic tape is coated with a magnetizable material. Each character is represented as a column of bits

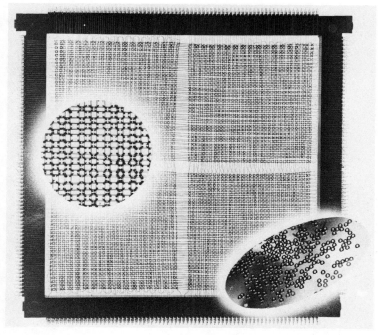

Fig. 12.1 (cont.)

across the tape. A read/write head for each channel or track senses the bits as the tape passes under it. Records are separated by an interrecord gap to define the end of the record and give space for stopping the tape after one operation and for accelerating it to the proper speed before the next operation begins. However, to save time, several records can be blocked between the gaps. (See Figure 12.2.) A tape with a density of 800 characters per inch and a speed of 18.75 inches per second is read at the rate of 15,000 characters per second. Punched cards are read at about 1,300 characters per second and punched at 300 characters per second.

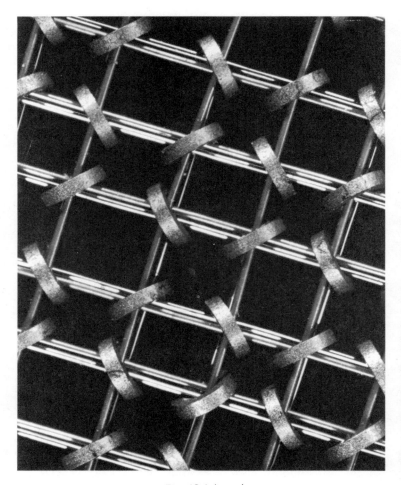

Fig. 12.1 (cont.)

Punched Cards

These have been described in Chapter 8. They are bulkier than magnetic tape—one tape can hold the equivalent of 400,000 punched cards at average recording densities. Magnetic

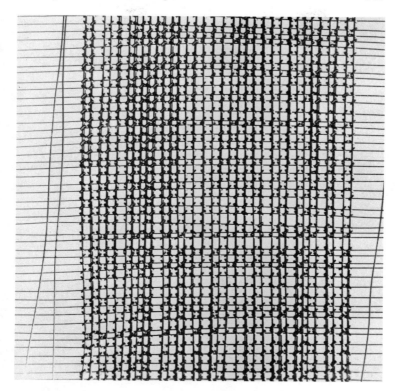

Fig. 12.1 (cont.)

tape, unlike punched cards, can also be reused, which makes the tape actually cheaper in the long run. Since magnetic tape can be read much faster than punched cards or paper tape, small computers or special off-line card-to-tape converters are often used to transfer information from cards or paper tape to magnetic tape.

The magnetic data recorder records data directly on magnetic tape without the intervening step of putting it on cards. (See Figure 12.3.)

Fig. 12.2. Tape measures progress at Michigan Blue Cross-Blue Shield where magnetic tape is placed in new Honeywell 800-III. The new reel is only ¾ inch wide and weighs only five pounds. The 26-pound, 3-inch reel (foreground) is from a D-1000 business computer, the first ever built by Honeywell. The D-1000 is being retired. (*Courtesy of Honeywell Inc.*)

Fig. 12.3. Honeywell's keytape devices bypass conventional punched card preparation by transcribing information directly onto magnetic tape from the keyboard. Typing and control functions are similar to those on a keypunch machine. (*Courtesy of Honeywell Inc.*)

Delay Lines

The early delay-line memory still has its uses. Delay lines are electronic circuits that include an element (such as a magnetostrictive device or glass element) which permits electric signals as a series of bits to travel at acoustic speeds. In the mercury delay line electric pulses are converted into the slower supersonic waves traveling through a column of mercury. The ends of the lines are connected so that the signals circulate continually; the line can be tapped for input and output. Delay lines appear at first to be cheap—a line that stores up to 20,000 bits may cost about half a cent a bit. However, the storage of data must be synchronized with the circulation of information, and the cost of the control circuits may outweigh the savings on the delay line proper.

Data Cells

The data cell is a random-access system of banks of magnetizable tape which can store millions of bytes. To read from the device, the cell specified by the program is positioned and a pie-shaped subcell is removed. From this a tape strip is in turn removed and wound around a drum supplied with a read/write head. This storage is slower and cheaper than disk storage, and is suited to handling large volumes of data.

CRAM

A CRAM (random access memory) unit contains a cartridge of several hundred large mylar magnetic cards that can be selected, placed on a rotating drum for reading or writing, and put back in place. It is suitable for large volumes of data.

Thin Films

Thin film memory is in effect a miniature system of magnetic cores. Access is fast because the unit is compact. This memory may also consist of small metallic deposits on plastic, glass, or ceramic plates. Very thin wires connect the deposited dots. In another type, magnetic thin film is plated on wires and insulated wires are woven around them. Each intersection of the two types of wire produces a bit.

Cryogenics

The resistance of metals drop rapidly as temperatures approach absolute zero, and the cryogenic memory utilizes this fact. At present the cost of the necessary refrigeration is prohibitive.

Experimental Techniques

Experiments are being made on laser memories and holographic memories. Another technique is the bubble memory, based on the fact that a magnetic field causes an alteration in a ferrite crystal. The particles affected can be less than half a mil in size. It is possible to control the reading in and out of this "bubble" within the crystal.

The cost of any memory technique depends not only on the storage medium itself but also on the cost of peripheral circuits and handling. With magnetic tape and magnetic disk the cost lies not in the medium, but in the mechanical devices for handling the motion of the tapes and disks. The cost is usually higher for memories that are addressable—that is, in which it is possible to find a wanted item directly by its location or address.

Memories that are not addressable, such as paper tape, punched cards, and most forms of magnetic tape, have sequential access—that is, an item can be read only after all the items that precede it have been scanned. Before data stored in sequential-access devices can be processed, it must be transferred to random-access storage such as core, disk, drum, and data cell units.

chapter 13

Processing a Program on a Computer

Central Processing Unit

In early computers separate designs were used for scientific and commercial computers. Scientific computers usually called for relatively few input-output operations and many processing steps. Processing speed was important, but raw (unedited) output was usually acceptable. Commercial computers had the reverse requirements. The output had to be clear and of high quality—it had to be edited for grouping, spacing, punctuation, and the use of dollar signs and other special marks.

This distinction is becoming blurred, and many computers are now built to serve a general purpose. The user of a computer such as the IBM System/360 has a wide range of speed and size to choose from in processors, and additional modules of main storage can often be added. Most computers can also have auxiliary storage in the form of tape or disks. Data from auxiliary storage has to be read into main storage before it can be processed, and the results have to be read out to the auxiliary unit if they are to be stored there.

A number of computers, including some models of the IBM System/370, offer virtual memory, which amounts to using a high-speed direct-access device (disk or drum) as if it were an expanded main processor storage. With it, storage addresses up to the logical limit of the system's addressing structure (in the 370, 16,777,216 bytes) can be directly used by programs independent of the actual size of the system's main storage.

The central processing unit (CPU) consists of the control unit and the arithmetic and logical unit (ALU). In general, the ALU contains the circuits for arithmetic operations such as add, subtract, multiply, and divide and the circuits for logical operations such as comparing, moving, bit testing, shifting, and editing.

Multiprocessing

Early computers were limited in the number of their input-output devices because each type of device required a different series of control signals, which had to flow across the boundary, or I/O interface, between the computer proper and the device. If the CPU has to handle instructions for many devices, it cannot keep up with the load. This problem was solved by using a standard interface, to which any kind of I/O device can be attached, and letting each type of I/O device use its own control unit, connected to a channel. A channel is a small computer that selects and executes programs held in main storage. One of these programs supplies the channel commands to the control unit. The channels thus relieve the CPU of the work of controlling the I/O devices. Once a CPU instruction has initiated a channel program, the CPU can return to processing. If necessary, it can interrupt processing to start another input operation. Processing and I/O operations are done concurrently, and a great variety of peripherals can be incorporated in a single computer system.

There are selector channels and multiplexer channels. A selector channel transmits all the bytes of information in one data record from an input device or to an output device in one

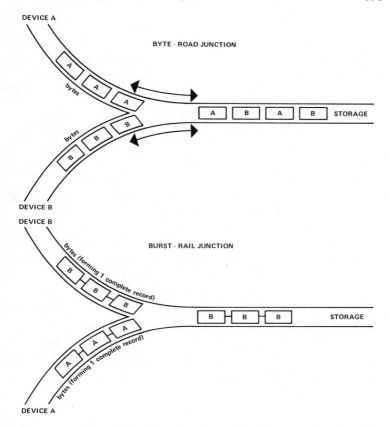

Fig. 13.1. Byte and burst transmission modes. (*Courtesy of IBM*)

operation—in so-called burst mode. A multiplexer channel can operate in burst mode, but it can also operate in byte mode, in which it transmits one byte of information at a time to or from storage. When it operates by byte mode, it may be connected to several I/O devices and transmit a byte of data first from one, then from the next, and so on, in what is called byte interleaving. (See Figure 13.1.)

In the IBM System/360 one multiplexer channel can be connected to control units for as many as 256 I/O devices, depending on the types of the devices. A large number of these devices can operate at the same time, so that one multiplexer channel can serve an entire system. Each selector channel can also address as many as 256 I/O devices but only one I/O device can use the channel at any one time, so that a system may have as many as six selector channels in addition to a multiplexer.

A system might have all selector channels reading or writing, or some reading and others writing, while the multiplexer was operating and the CPU was processing data. Overlap is possible with all the I/O devices and channels connected to the system. Reading, processing, and writing in the CPU can also be overlapped for increasing efficiency. In overlapping, one storage area is used for reading in or writing out data and another area for processing. This scheme is called buffering. The dedicated or buffer storage area is not a separate piece of hardware but is part of main storage. The programmer sets aside and specifies the buffer areas. Data in a buffer may be processed where it is or moved elsewhere for computation.

Program Execution

A control program (sometimes called the supervisor) is a special program that always resides in main storage. A problem or application program causes the computer to perform the operations necessary to do a specific job, such as calculating a payroll. Some problem programs are supplied by the manufacturer and some are written by the user.

One of the functions of the supervisor is to locate problem programs in auxiliary storage and load them into main storage in a sequence dictated by the punched job cards. The supervisor also controls and coordinates the I/O functions for all problem programs. When a job is being processed, main storage always contains a supervisor program and a problem program. The CPU executes instructions from the supervisor or the problem program according to which program is in control at the moment. The CPU status changes from the so-called problem state to the supervisor state when the problem program requests an I/O operation. After the I/O operation has been initiated, the supervisor returns the CPU to the problem program. When some exceptional condition arises, a signal called an interrupt is generated, which is in fact a request for a change in the status of the CPU. For instance, an I/O operation may be taking place while a problem program is being processed. The end of an I/O operation is considered to be an exceptional condition, and an interrupt signal will be generated. The System/360 also has an external interrupt (initiated by the operator), which is used for program check, machine check, and supervisor call.

A program status word (PSW) is a doubleword the contents of which show the logical status of the computer with respect to the program being executed—for instance, the program state of the CPU and the address of the next instruction to be executed.

The Operating System

The system residence device is an auxiliary storage unit that holds a file of programs that together make up the operating system for the computer. One of these is the supervisor. As these programs are needed, they are called into main storage to be executed. The residence is usually a magnetic disk unit because it offers direct access to the selected program. The core image library is a section of the residence from which programs can be loaded directly into main storage. All the elements of these programs (instructions, storage and work areas, and so forth) have been assigned the actual main storage addresses they will occupy and thus may be said to be in "core image."

Before a computer can do anything, the supervisor must be transferred to main storage. This is done by means of the initial program loader (IPL) program, which the operator at the console can extract from the system residence manually and load into main storage. The IPL then locates and loads the supervisor. Other programs are loaded by the system loader, which is part of the supervisor.

A job is the basic independent unit of work done by the operating system. If the job is a COBOL compile run, the job program will be a COBOL compiler. The input for the job is the source program written in COBOL. The output is an object program in machine language. The output can be written directly on the system residence device or on some other medium such as cards.

The librarian is a program composed of special routines that maintain, service, and organize the libraries of the operating system. Each library has a directory, that is, a list of the programs and their library addresses. Programs that need access to other programs in the library must consult the proper directory to find the address and length of the program wanted.

System/360 offers several operating systems, each adapted to the needs of a certain group of users. The OS (Operating System) offers the maximum in I/O device support and other capabilities. In general, the more powerful the operating system, the more main storage it takes up. The BOS (Basic Operating System) would be adequate for a user who has a small System/360 with disk units and needs only Assembler Language or RPG. The TOS (Tape Operating System) would serve a user who has a system without disk files, but who needs the support of all languages plus multiprogramming, storage protection, and an interval timer.

chapter 14

Coding

The Binary System

In the Chapter 5 we explained that instead of the decimal system, the computer uses the binary system because it has only two states—ON or OFF.

To understand how the binary system works, let's look at the decimal system. In the end right-hand column (which is called the least significant) we can do our adding up to 9; when we add another 1, we put a zero in this column and a 1 in the next column to show that we have gone through the least significant column one time. And when we get up to 10 in this second column, we put a 0 in the second column and a 1 in the third column to show we have gone through the second column one time; and we get 100.

We do the same sort of thing in the binary system, but instead of waiting to put a 1 in the second column until we have gone past 9 in the first column, *we put a 1 in the second column every time we go past 1 in the first column.* In other words, we have only two digits—0 and 1. We write a 2 by putting a 1 in the second column, thus: 1 0. If we now want to add 1 to this number, we do it just as we do in the decimal system, and put a 1 in the least significant column: 1 1. When we want to add another 1, the least significant column goes back to 0 and the total of that column is represented by a carry to the next column. That makes this next column 2, which we represent by 0 and a carry, just as we represent 10 by 0 and a carry in the decimal system. So we end up with 1 0 0, which is equal to 4 in the binary system.

It is obvious that if we are going to use fewer different characters in each column, we are going to get more columns —we have counted only up to 4 and we already have three columns. When we get up to 8, which is still in the first decimal column, we need four columns in binary: 1 0 0 0. And in binary the number 19 takes five columns: 1 0 0 1 1.

This looks like a very unhandy system for counting sheep or doing your income tax. But it has one great advantage: we can record a binary number with anything that goes OFF and ON if we say that whenever the thing is OFF, it represents 0 and whenever it is on, it represents 1. We can now use not only a vacuum tube, but a flashlight, an Indian smoke signal, or even blinks of the eyes. Or we can record binary numbers on tape by punching or not punching a hole. (See Figure 14.1.)

Besides the decimal system (base 10) and binary system (base 2) we should mention the octal system (base 8) and the hexadecimal system (base 16). There is a very handy relationship between the binary system and these two new systems.

If we group the binary digits in a binary number by threes, they correspond, and convert, to octal digits. For example, to change 011001111100 to octal, beginning at the right, group the binary digits in threes:

$$011 \quad 001 \quad 111 \quad 100$$

Three binary digits never represent more than 7 (111). Therefore they transfer over to the octal system without the necessity for a carry.

$$011 \quad 001 \quad 111 \quad 100$$
$$3 \qquad 1 \qquad 7 \qquad 4$$

DECIMAL			BINARY			
t e n s	u n i t s		e i g h t s	f o u r s	t w o s	u n i t s
0	0		0	0	0	0
0	1		0	0	0	1
0	2		0	0	1	0
0	3		0	0	1	1
0	4		0	1	0	0
0	5		0	1	0	1
0	6		0	1	1	0
0	7		0	1	1	1
0	8		1	0	0	0
0	9		1	0	0	1
1	0		1	0	1	0
1	1		1	0	1	1
1	2		1	1	0	0
1	3		1	1	0	1
1	4		1	1	1	0
1	5		1	1	1	1

Fig. 14.1. Decimal and binary systems.

161

All the possible binary triplets (000 through 111) convert to all of the possible octal digits (0 through 7).

Binary	Octal
000	0
001	1
010	2
011	3
100	4
101	5
110	6
111	7

To convert 356 in octal to decimal:

$$3 \times 8^2 \quad = 192$$
$$5 \times 8^1 \quad = \ 40$$
$$6 \qquad\quad = \underline{\ \ 6}$$
$$238$$

In the same way four binary digits never add up to more than 15 (1111), so that binary digits can be grouped in fours and converted to hexadecimal digits without a carry.

The 16 digits in the hexadecimal number system are 0, 1, 2, 3, 4, 5, 6, 7, 8, 9, A, B, C, D, E, F. We use A to represent 10, B for 11, C for 12, D for 13, E for 14, and F for 15 because the numbers 10, 11, 12, 13, 14, 15 are not digits, but combinations of two digits each, and their use as digits would be confusing.

In the hexadecimal system, column or place values begin at 1 and increase by factors of 16 as we go from right to left.

$$16^2 \quad 16^1 \quad 16^0$$
$$256 \quad 16 \quad \ 1$$

The hexadecimal number $(2A4)_{16}$ can be charted as

$$256 \quad 16 \quad 1$$
$$2 \quad A \quad 4$$

and converted:

$$2 \times 256 = 512$$
$$10 \times \ 16 = 160$$
$$4 \times \ \ 1 = \ \ \underline{4}$$
$$676$$

The Punched Card Code

The standard IBM card has 80 vertical columns and 12 horizontal columns. (See Figure 14.2.) In the Hollerith code, any digit from 0 through 9 is recorded by punching a hole through the digit in the column wanted. These are numeric punches. Letters are represented by two punches in the same column. One of the two punches is a nonzero numeric punch and the other is a zone punch. The zone punches are in lines 11, 12, and 0 (the last doubles as a numerical punch and a zone punch.) (Figure 14.3.)

EBCDIC

A bit is a binary digit, or the information contained in the choice between 1 and 0. A byte is a group or set of bits, usually 8. The System/360 can store whole numbers as 32-bit fullwords (we also have 16-bit halfwords, and 64-bit doublewords) where the bits represent the equivalent of the decimal number being stored.

Each 32-bit word can also be considered as four eight-bit bytes. If we use each byte to represent one character (letter, digit, or special character), we have a handy way of representing

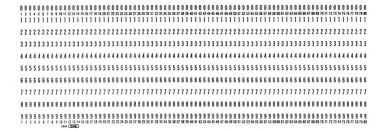

Fig. 14.2. Punched card.

names, addresses, and other strings of alphanumeric characters. (Data that consists of letters, digits, and special characters is called alphanumeric.)

One code that uses eight bits to represent each character is called the Extended Binary Coded Decimal Interchange Code, or EBCDIC.

Character	EBCDIC (binary)
0	1111 0000
1	1111 0001
2	1111 0010
3	1111 0011
4	1111 0100
5	1111 0101
6	1111 0110
7	1111 0111
8	1111 1000
9	1111 1001

The binary equivalent of each digit appears as the last four bits of the byte. However, all eight bits are necessary since all characters must be the same size, and for the 360 that size is one byte or eight bits.

In the figure the bit configuration is shown for each character as two sets of four bits each. This is done here to make the code easier to read. It also leads to the use of hexadecimal

Character	Card Punches
0	0
1	1
2	2
3	3
4	4
5	5
6	6
7	7
8	8
9	9
A	12 - 1
B	12 - 2
C	12 - 3
D	12 - 4
E	12 - 5
F	12 - 6
G	12 - 7
H	12 - 8
I	12 - 9
J	11 - 1
K	11 - 2
L	11 - 3
M	11 - 4
N	11 - 5
O	11 - 6
P	11 - 7
Q	11 - 8
R	11 - 9
S	0 - 2
T	0 - 3
U	0 - 4
V	0 - 5
W	0 - 6
X	0 - 7
Y	0 - 8
Z	0 - 9

Fig. 14.3. The punched card code.

shorthand: one hex digit for every four binary digits, two hex digits for each eight-bit character.

Character	*EBCDIC (binary)*	*EBCDIC (hex)*
0	1111 0000	F0
1	1111 0001	F1
2	1111 0010	F2
3	1111 0011	F3
4	1111 0100	F4
5	1111 0101	F5
6	1111 0110	F6
7	1111 0111	F7
8	1111 1000	F8
9	1111 1001	F9

To represent only numeric characters we could use the four-bit code and let each byte represent two numeric characters. But to represent letters and special characters as well as digits, we need more than four bits to code all 10 digits and all 26 letters, plus the special characters.

The code for the letters is shown on the following page. The relationship between the EBCDIC code and the Hollerith code is apparent. The EBCDIC format for character data represents digits in a so-called zoned decimal format with one character per byte. Suppose we stand a byte (8 bits) on end. Bit 0 will be at the top and bit 7 at the bottom as shown in this illustration:

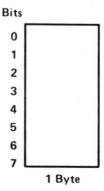

Character	EBCDIC (binary)	EBCDIC (hex)
A	1100 0001	C1
B	1100 0010	C2
C	1100 0011	C3
D	1100 0100	C4
E	1100 0101	C5
F	1100 0110	C6
G	1100 0111	C7
H	1100 1000	C8
I	1100 1001	C9
J	1101 0001	D1
K	1101 0010	D2
L	1101 0011	D3
M	1101 0100	D4
N	1101 0101	D5
O	1101 0110	D6
P	1101 0111	D7
Q	1101 1000	D8
R	1101 1001	D9
S	1110 0010	E2
T	1110 0011	E3
U	1110 0100	E4
V	1110 0101	E5
W	1110 0110	E6
X	1110 0111	E7
Y	1110 1000	E8
Z	1110 1001	E9

Now divide the byte in half by drawing a line across it. If we label the top half ZONE and the bottom half DIGIT, we can readily see the resemblance between the byte and a card. Four bits must be used to represent the decimal digits 0–9. In EBCDIC, a 12-zone is represented by a hexadecimal (hex) C, an 11-zone by a hex D, a zero-zone by a hex E and a no-zone by a hex F.

$$\text{hex } C = 1100$$
$$\text{hex } D = 1101$$

hex E = 1110
hex F = 1111

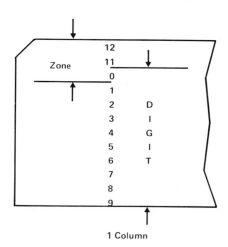

We have been showing the byte in a vertical position for convenience of comparison with the card data format. The byte may represent data in other formats. Some of these formats require more than one byte. Because of these additional requirements, it is conventional to show the bytes strung out end to end.

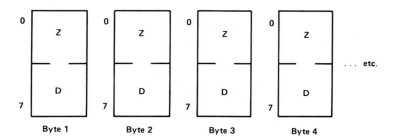

Conventionally, these bytes are shown like this:

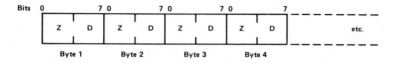

In addition the bit structure within a byte is represented by two hexadecimal digits.

The hexadecimal representation of the following characters:

F	9	F	7	C	4

would be

1111	1001	1111	0111	1100	0100

We have been working with unsigned numbers. Generally, unsigned numbers are assumed to be positive. But in many cases numbers may be positive or negative, and to distinguish one from the other, plus and minus signs are used. In S/360 the sign of a number is stored as the zone portion of the low-order byte. Negative numbers are indicated by a hex D. Hex D corresponds to the 11-punch in punch card practice. Thus, a -17 looks like this:

F	1	D	7

All other zones (hex C, E and F) are always assumed positive.

In S/360, the zoned decimal numbers must be in another format for the variable-field-length arithmetic and edit operations. This format is called the "packed" format. Here the flexible byte may be used to store two digits. Packed decimal format provides increased arithmetic performance and improved rate of data transmission. The hex representation of 5796 in zoned decimal is:

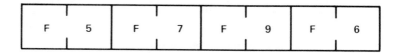

In packed format the zones are removed from the numbers (except for the low-order number) and then the numbers are compressed (packed) into a shorter field. In the previous example, packing produces this result:

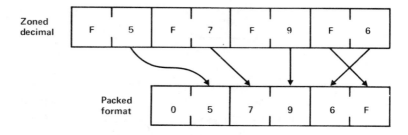

Three actions occur:

    1. The numbers are packed from 4 bytes into 3 bytes.

    2. In the low-order byte, the zone and digit are interchanged.

    3. Any unfilled high-order portions in the packed field are padded with zeros.

Characters	EBCDIC (hex)	ASCII (hex)
A	C1	A1
B	C2	A2
C	C3	A3
D	C4	A4
E	C5	A5
F	C6	A6
G	C7	A7
H	C8	A8
I	C9	A9
J	D1	AA
K	D2	AB
L	D3	AC
M	D4	AD
N	D5	AE
O	D6	AF
P	D7	B0
Q	D8	B1
R	D9	B2
S	E2	B3
T	E3	B4
U	E4	B5
V	E5	B6
W	E6	B7
X	E7	B8
Y	E8	B9
Z	E9	BA
0	F0	50
1	F1	51
2	F2	52
3	F3	53
4	F4	54
5	F5	55
6	F6	56
7	F7	57
8	F8	58
9	F9	59

171

In the zone decimal number format, the sign of the number is stored in the zone portion of the low-order digit. Action 2 thus provides us with a means of retaining the sign of the number in a PACK operation.

ASCII

The American Standard Code for Information Interchange, or ASCII, is an attempt to provide a standard for the interchange of coded information among various types of computing equipment. Such a standard is becoming more necessary as such equipment is more extensively linked together by data transmission. The ASCII code for the letters A through Z is a continuous code in hexadecimal. The EBCDIC code corresponds with the Hollerith zone-numeric code as shown on page 171.

In the System/360 the internal storage is in the form of eight-bit bytes. Each byte also has a ninth bit, a parity bit, used to check for machine errors.

The extra parity bit is determined to be 1 or 0, according to which will make the total number of 1-bits odd. The byte is then checked every time it is used. If the total number of 1-bits becomes even, the operator at the console is notified that there is a parity error.

EBCDIC Tape Code

Magnetic tape is a flexible plastic tape coated on one side with an iron compound that can be magnetized. Different System/360 tape drives record data in seven or nine tracks on the tape. In both types data is recorded across the tape. The nine-track EBCDIC tape code is shown on page 173.

Character	9-Track EBCDIC Code
0	0-1-2-3
1	P-0-1-2-3-7
2	P-0-1-2-3-6
3	0-1-2-3-6-7
4	P-0-1-2-3-5
5	0-1-2-3-5-7
6	0-1-2-3-5-6
7	P-0-1-2-3-5-6-7
8	P-0-1-2-3-4
9	0-1-2-3-4-7
A	P-0-1-7
B	P-0-1-6
C	0-1-6-7
D	P-0-1-5
E	0-1-5-7
F	0-1-5-6
G	P-0-1-5-6-7
H	P-0-1-4
I	0-1-4-7
J	0-1-3-7
K	0-1-3-6
L	P-0-1-3-6-7
M	0-1-3-5
N	P-0-1-3-5-7
O	P-0-1-3-5-6
P	0-1-3-5-6-7
Q	0-1-3-4
R	P-0-1-3-4-7
S	0-1-2-6
T	P-0-1-2-6-7
U	0-1-2-5
V	P-0-1-2-5-7
W	P-0-1-2-5-6
X	0-1-2-5-6-7
Y	0-1-2-4
Z	P-0-1-2-4-7

Tracks 4, 5, 6, and 7 together indicate the second digit of the two-digit EBCDIC code. The values of these four tracks are respectively 8, 4, 2, 1. The tracks are selected so as to add up to the value of the second digit.

When necessary, specified bits indicate whether a number is positive or negative.

Floating-Point Arithmetic

Another problem is representing a number that is too big for a fixed-length field. For example, the largest positive integer than can be represented in binary in a 32-bit word is 2,147,483,647, or a little more than 2×10^9. We get around this by using floating-point arithmetic—that is, by moving the decimal point around. With floating-point we can represent $+7 \times 10^{75}$ in a 32-bit word.

A floating-point number has two parts, an exponent and a fraction. We can thus represent a decimal number as a decimal fraction times a power of 10:

$$373.645 = .373645 \times 10^3$$
$$27.56 \quad = .2756 \times 10^2$$
$$.0099 \quad = .99 \times 10^{-2}$$

Either the exponent or the fraction can be positive or negative.

$$+.00746 \quad = -2, +.746$$
$$-1744.223 = +4, -.1744223$$

System/360 performs its floating-point arithmetic in hexadecimal. Decimal numbers used in calculations must first be converted to hexadecimal and then put in floating-point form.

When this is done, the fraction is a series of hexadecimal digits to the right of a hexadecimal point, and the exponent is a power of 16.

Forms of Instructions

On a punched card a number of consecutive columns are often reserved for specific kinds of information such as name, address, and social security number. These reserved sections are called fields. Instructions to a computer may be represented in three forms—actual, symbolic, and explicit. The actual or machine-language form is the form in which the instruction is stored in the computer. This is the output of the language translator programs and is never written by the programmer. The symbolic instruction identifies the field by some expression (label) that has a meaning in English, such as SALARY, OVERTIME, TAX. An explicit instruction is one in which the address and length of a field (in bytes) are explicitly coded by the programmer.

We might have:

Symbolic coding — AP THERE,HERE
Explicit   coding — AP 17(5, 11), 473(4, 11)

The two instructions will generate exactly equivalent machine instructions in the program.

Programming

The computer processes data according to a list of instructions. Both the data and the instructions must be in the computer's memory while the processing is going on. The

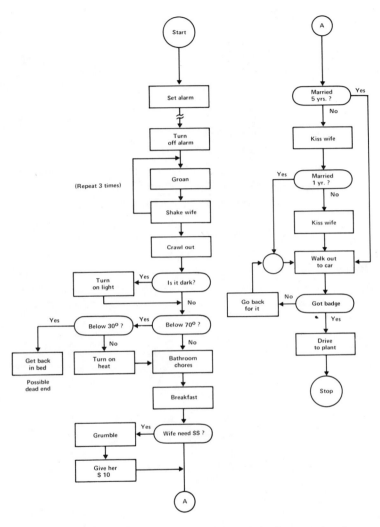

Fig. 14.4. Flowchart: "How to get to work in the morning."

176

programmer prepares the list of instructions, or program, to be entered into the computer. After the operator starts the computer, the entire program will usually be gone through without any further help from the operator.

Programming involves several steps. First the programmer must decide on the best way to solve it by computer. Then he makes a flowchart, or diagram, of the logic of the solution. (See Figure 14.4.) Only then does he write the series of instructions in a form the computer can handle. But his work is not yet over. He must debug the program—that is, run it on a computer to discover and correct any mistakes in logic or coding. He must document the program as he goes along—that is, prepare a description of the problem, note the language and the computer he used, put in the flowchart, and write out any special operating instructions that will be useful to somebody else who may want to use or modify the program.

chapter 15

Languages

Every computer comes equipped with a specific set of instructions that it can execute. The actual set of symbols that the computer hardware can interpret is the direct machine language for that computer. Since most computers operate on binary bits, the machine language is usually binary. An instruction might look like this:

001101 000000 010100 000000 010000 000000

In the early days the programmer had to write the program in this unhandy machine language and mistakes were easy to make. The first improvement came when the instruction itself was written in mnemonic or easily remembered code. Thus the first six digits of the instruction above might be given as ADD, but the rest or address part of the instruction would remain in binary.

Later on the address part of the instruction was written in decimal form. But the difficulty remained that when an actual address for a storage location was given, the addition or elimination of a single instruction or piece of data might change the sequence for all the rest of the addresses and make it necessary to change all of them. Relative addressing, in which the program was divided into sections and addresses were given from the start of a section, was somewhat better.

Finally completely symbolic notation and addressing were devised for both instructions and data. The Whirlwind binary computer, developed at MIT in 1947–51, used numeric symbolic addresses. Then mnemonic symbols came into use for both instructions and data. In ADD TAX, for instance, TAX would stand for the location of a variable, tax.

It soon became clear that it would be useful to have a standard set of symbols instead of letting each programmer make up his own. Programmers could thus use one another's work, in particular standard routines for square root and other such computations. A library of written programs could be built up. Programmers also wanted more natural notation.

One of the first meetings held to discuss what was then called automatic programming took place in 1954, and since then programming languages have mushroomed. The difficulty with them is that, like English, they are alive and changing, and by the time a language is written down in some agreed standard, it is already out of date, like the dictionary.

There are various levels of computer language. The basic level, as we have seen, is the machine code—the one the computer itself understands. The next level above, assembler language, is called lower level because it represents the operations of the computer rather than the more complex concepts of business or scientific operations. In assembler language, one instruction causes one computation or movement of data in the computer—that is, there is a one-to-one correspondence between an assembler language and a machine language. In a higher-level language, one instruction normally creates more than one machine instruction. For instance, an instruction might state ADD A TO B. This operation requires more than one machine instruction for execution.

Programs in symbolic languages such as FORTRAN must be translated into machine language by a compiler. The program written by the programmer is the source program and the program that results from the translation is the object program. There must be a different compiler for each language and each machine code. But it is often possible to take the same program written in a higher-level language and run it through two different compiler programs designed for two different computers, and come up with an object program for each computer. Thus jobs can be transferred from one computer to another. Some languages, such as COBOL and FORTRAN, may be used to write source programs for execution on computers made by different manufacturers.

To write a program in a programming language, the programmer does not have to know the computer's machine code, or indeed much of anything about the computer, such as whether numbers are represented internally in binary or hexadecimal. However, he should know what facilities the computer offers, such as mass storage and I/O equipment, and he will be more efficient if he knows something about the registers available and the number representation.

When a compiler program converts a source program to an object program, it allocates storage for I/O areas, assigns storage locations to data referred to in the source statements by symbolic names, creates machine language instructions from the source language and assigns storage addresses to them, and builds into the machine instructions the addresses of the data they will process. The compiler program also produces a source listing and a cross-reference listing for testing and documentation.

Languages may be machine oriented or problem oriented. A machine-oriented language permits the programmer to specify exactly which machine features he wants to use at designated points in the program. A problem-oriented language leaves it to the compiler to select the machine features to be used and specify where to use them.

Some languages are free form—they permit the programmer to write his source statements in narrative style instead of according to a definite format.

Report Program Generator (RPG) was developed to provide a language that would quickly develop programs to print reports.

Common Business Oriented Language (COBOL) was designed for commercial problems. Its source language statements resemble English rather than mathematical expressions and coding is more or less free form. Like RPG, COBOL is problem oriented. It is manufacturer compatible; a source program in COBOL can be compiled and run on any computer, regardless of the manufacturer, if there is a compiler for the system in question.

Formula Translation (FORTRAN) is in wide use for coding scientific and engineering problems. Its source statements resemble mathematical expressions rather than English, and it is partially restricted in form. It is high level, problem oriented, and manufacturer compatible.

Programming Language One (PL/1) was developed for System/360. It was designed to bridge the gap between scientific languages such as FORTRAN and commercial languages such as COBOL by offering features of both, since the distinction between commercial and scientific computing is becoming blurred.

Beginner's All-Purpose Symbolic Instruction Code (BASIC) lacks some of the capability of the complete FORTRAN language, which it resembles, but it can be learned much faster. It is popular among laymen who want to do their own programming and computing, and is widely used in time sharing.

Algorithmic Language (ALGOL) resembles FORTRAN and PL/1 and is intended for mathematical problems. A similar language is JOVIAL (Jules' Own Version of the International Algebraic Language).

And SNOBOL, LISP, SLIP, COMIT, and IPL-V are designed for string manipulation or list processing. These languages consist of a set of rules, or statements, which assist in processing strings of characters.

SIMSCRIPT is somewhat like FORTRAN and is designed for programming simulations. It can be used to break up complex mathematical models to a series of interrelated smaller components.

IBM COBOL PROGRAM SHEET

Form No. X28-1464-2 U/M 050 Printed in U. S. A.

System		Punching Instructions	Sheet of
Program	Graphic	Card Form# *	Identification
Programmer / Date	Punch		73 — 80

SEQUENCE (PAGE) 1 3 (SERIAL) 4 6 | CONT. 7 | A 8 | B 12 16 20 24 28 32 36 40 44 48 52 56 60 64 68 72

```
01 PROCEDURE DIVISION.
02
03 START-PROCESSING. OPEN INPUT BILLING-FILE, OUTPUT
04     CUSTOMER-BILL-FILE.
05
06 READ-AND-CHECK-RECORD. READ BILLING-FILE; AT END, GO TO
07     END-OF-RUN. IF NUMBER-OF-TRANSACTIONS IN THIS-MONTH IS
08     EQUAL TO ZERO, OR CURRENT-BALANCE IS NEGATIVE, GO TO
09     READ-AND-CHECK-RECORD.
10
11 LINE-1-PROCEDURE. MOVE SPACES TO BILL-LINE-1. MOVE
12     BALANCE-FORWARD TO OLD-BALANCE. MOVE AMOUNT OF PURCHASES IN
13     THIS-MONTH TO PURCHASES IN BILL-LINE-1. MOVE AMOUNT OF
14     PAYMENTS IN THIS-MONTH TO PAYMENTS IN BILL-LINE-1. MOVE
15     AMOUNT OF CREDITS IN THIS-MONTH TO CREDITS IN BILL-LINE-1.
16     MOVE ACCOUNT-NUMBER OF BILLING-RECORD TO ACCOUNT-NUMBER IN
17     BILL-LINE-1. MOVE BILLING-DATE OF THIS-MONTH TO BILLING-DATE
18     IN BILL-LINE-1.
19
20
```

* A standard card form, IBM electro C61897, is available for punching source statements from this form.

Fig. 15.1. COBOL Program Sheet.

Table 15.1. Printed Code.

*LOC	OBJECT CODE	ADDR1	ADDR2	STMT	SOURCE STATEMENT		COMMENTS
0005B4	4199 0004		00004	100+IJFVOUB	LA	IJFVRC,4(IJFVRC)	INCREASE BLOCKSIZE BY FOUR
0005B8	4560 F184		006DC	101+	BAL	IJFVRA,IJFVEX1	
0005BC	1B99			102+	SR	IJFVRC,IJFVRC	ZERO BLOCKSIZE
0005BE	47F0 F03C		00594	103+	B	IJFVEX3	GO TO EXIT
0005C2	906E F318		00870	104+IJFVGET	STM	IJFVRA,IJFVRH,IJFVSAV	SAVE USER REGISTERS
0005C6	9889 1048		00048	105+	LM	IJFVRB,IJFVRC,IJFVDB3	PICK UP CURRENT I/O AND BLCKSZ
0005CA	9180 1015	00015		106+	TM	IJFVSWI,IJFVOPN	TEST IF FIRST TIME
0005CE	4780 F08E		005E6	107+	BZ	IJFVGTR	YES READ A BLOCK
0005D2	4560 F16A		006C2	108+	BAL	IJFVRA,IJFVDBL	GO TO DEBLOCKING ROUTINE
0005D6	5590 1058		00058	109+	CL	IJFVRC,IJFVDB6	TEST IF END OF BLOCK
0005DA	47A0 F08E		005E6	110+	BC	10,IJFVGTR	YES GO TO READ NEW BLOCK
0005DE	4570 F0F8		00650	111+IJFVSTW	BAL	IJFVRV,IJFVWRK	GO TO WORKAREA SUBROUTINE
0005E2	47F0 F03C		00594	112+	B	IJFVEX3	GO TO EXIT
0005E6	4890 105C		0005C	113+IJFVGTR	LH	IJFVRC,IJFVBZ1	LOAD BLOCKSIZE TO REGISTER
0005EA	4560 F184		006DC	114+	BAL	IJFVRA,IJFVEX1	GO TO ROUTINE TO READ BLOCK
0005EE	1B9A			115+IJFVGTB	SR	IJFVRC,IJFVRD	SUBTR. RES. COUNT FROM BLOCKZ
0005F0	D201 1054 8000	00054	00000	116+	MVC	IJFVDB1(2),0(IJFVRB)	MOVE BLKSIZE IN RECORD READ
0005F6	4990 1054		00054	117+	CH	IJFVRC,IJFVDB1	AND COMPARE IT WITH ACTUAL BLC
0005FA	41E0 1064		00064	118+	LA	IJFVRH,IJFVWLR	LOAD WLR-ADDR TO REGISTER
0005FE	4770 F208		00760	119+	BNE	IJFVER1	IF COMPARE NE GO TO ERR.EXIT

*LOC—Storage addresses of machine language instructions.
OBJECT CODE—Machine language instructions in hexadecimal notation.
ADDR1 and ADDR2—Actual storage addresses of instruction operands.
STMT—Sequential number assigned to source program statement by compiler.
SOURCE STATEMENT—Source program statements, including labels, operation codes, and programmer comments.

chapter 16

Data Communications

Computers no longer sit and mull over their problems by themselves; they talk with one another—often, like people, by picking up the telephone and dialing a number. The techniques of data processing have now been wedded to the techniques of communications to form the new art of data communications. This has happened because the widely scattered plants and offices of modern corporations need to exchange information in a hurry. The last few years have seen an astonishing development of reliable medium- and high-speed terminal and communications processing equipment, together with reasonably priced standard communications facilities and flexible common-carrier services, so that any company can put together a system to suit its needs from components on the market.

Electrical data communications systems have in fact been around ever since Samuel Morse invented the telegraph in 1844. Torn-tape telegraph systems, which transmit data at around 10 characters per second, are still adequate for certain purposes, but faster equipment has become necessary since industry has seen the advantages of company-wide data-communications networks and the related concepts of real-time data processing and integrated management information systems. In fact AT&T expects that the volume of digital data transmitted will eventually equal the volume of voice transmission.

In a data-communications system each unit performs a specific function or functions determined by the needs of the system. Figure 16.1 shows the data flow between two terminals in a typical system. The input device may be a keyboard, paper-tape reader, card reader, magnetic tape unit, or computer. The output device may be a tape punch, card punch, printer, magnetic tape unit, display device, or computer. Before the data from the input device gets to the other end of the line, it must be handled by an input control, error control, synchronizer, modulator, communications line, demodulator, another synchronizer, another error control, and an output control. Several of these units are usually housed in one cabinet and marketed as a single device.

A communications facility or carrier may be telephone and telegraph cables, high-frequency radio, or line-of-sight microwave. The types most used at present are the standard public telephone and telegraph lines.

Control Units

The input control unit controls and accepts data from the input device at the speed of the device, stores the data temporarily, and transmits it at a rate compatible with that of the communications facility. At the other end the process is reversed. When no buffers are used, the input, data transmission, and output functions must proceed simultaneously and at the same speed. In more complex systems the I/O control units at the processing or switching centers are likely to be multiline controllers or even stored-program communications processors which can buffer and control simultaneous I/O transmission on many different lines. Error control techniques can be designed merely to detect and indicate errors, or also to correct certain types of errors. (See Figure 16.2.)

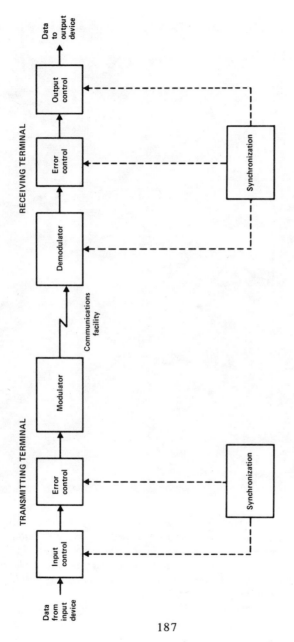

Fig. 16.1. Data flow in a typical data communications system.

187

Fig. 16.2. The DEC comm 11D24 programmable front end processor for IBM 360/370 computers relieves the host computer in a teleprocessing network of many data communications tasks such as line control, message switching, error control, code conversion, and message concentration. (*Courtesy of Digital Equipment Corporation*)

188

Synchronization Units

Data signal bits are transmitted at precise time intervals, and the transmitting and receiving stations must be synchronized. In the start/stop technique additional signals transmitted with each unit of data mark its beginning and end. In the synchronous transmission technique the bit configuration of a specific character is used to adjust the synchronizing circuitry to the transmitted bit rate.

Modulation-Demodulation Units

Carrier techniques were developed originally for telephone multiplex transmission and are the basis of radio. The constant-level (DC) pulses of the telegraph are replaced by data signals that vary regularly with time, establishing a transmission frequency. Equipment can be designed to isolate different frequencies so that multiple independent data paths can exist on the same line at the same time. The common carriers now pack many voice and/or data channels into a single broadband communications facility. Various techniques are used to modify the basic frequency signal.

When carrier techniques are used, it is necessary to convert the DC pulses generated by most data communications equipment into signals suitable for transmission. This is done by a modulation-demodulation unit, also called a modem or data set.

Applications

Data communications systems are now being put to use in six general ways:

Data collection from outlying facilities.

Data distribution to one or more outlying locations.

Processing inquiries from outlying locations (receiving an inquiry and sending an answer).

Balancing computer loads between the slack time in one computer's schedule and the peak load in another's, or providing backup in cases of breakdown.

Computer time sharing, or the simultaneous use of a computational facility by more than one person, each remote from the computer. There are two basic types —conversational time sharing and remote batch processing.

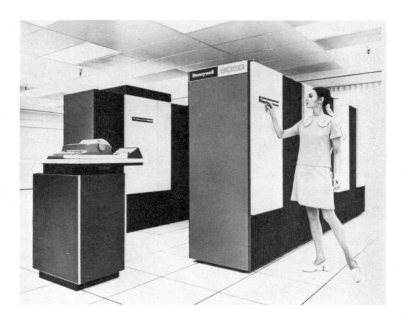

Fig. 16.3. Largest computer from Honeywell Information Systems is this Model 6080, which simultaneously handles time-sharing, remote batch processing, local processing, and transaction applications. (*Courtesy of Honeywell Inc.*)

(See Figure 16.3.) Both use multiple consoles connected to the central computer by communications links. Batch processing systems handle large programs that must be run to completion. Conversational systems usually have keyboards on the terminals. Turnaround time is short.

Message switching by computer, which is required when communications traffic is high. Here there is two-way message traffic between a number of terminals and a central switching center. The center gets each message from a sending terminal, stores it temporarily, does any necessary processing or code conversion, and then retransmits it to one or more designated receiving terminals. Large networks

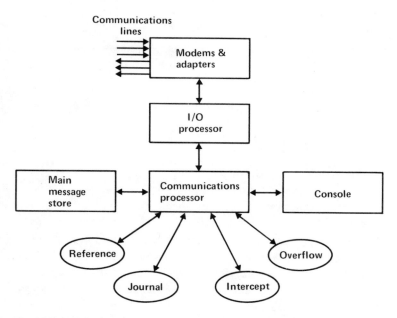

Fig. 16.4. A typical message-switching center. (*Courtesy of Honeywell Inc.*)

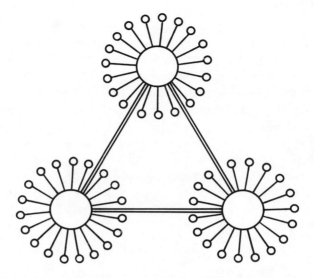

Fig. 16.5. Communications network including three interconnected
switching centers.

may use more than one switching center. (See Figures 16.4,
16.5.)

Need for New Facilities

Data communications have been hampered by what has
been called "an almost blind faith in public telephone systems as
a foundation for data communications requirements." Data
communications will not come into its own until digital transmission networks are developed which are specifically designed
to handle the requirements of data traffic. In the United States a
number of independent firms have asked the Federal Communications Commission for permission to build data transmission systems that use microwave links. Datran, Western
Union, Microwave Communications Inc. (MCI), and other
companies are entering the field.

chapter 17

Cathode-Ray Tube Displays, Microphotography, and Computer Output Microfilming

Computer output microfilming (COM) represents the confluence of the computer mainstream with two tributaries, the cathode-ray tube (CRT) and microphotography.

The CRT was the joined with the computer before microphotography was added.

Cathode-Ray Tube Displays

In 1879 Sir William Crookes experimented with electric discharges within gases and developed the Crookes tube, from which the modern CRT evolved. The first important use of the CRT was for oscillography, in which a pattern of electric signals can be seen on the CRT screen. In World War II oscilloscopes were quickly adapted to radar. Radar uses the CRT to show the reflections of electromagnetic signals from targets, which appear on the CRT screen as irregularities or bright spots. Television transmission soon followed—the face of the CRT was scanned continuously, and variations in its intensity formed a picture in real time. TV was demonstrated at the New York World's Fair in 1939.

By 1950, when the electronic computer was five years old, its greatest difficulty was becoming clear—the disparity between the speed of computer processing and the speed of the input and output of data. Feeding punched cards to a computer is about like feeding peanuts to an elephant one at a time. As for output, even in its infancy the computer was churning data at a rate approaching 100,000 characters per second, and an impact printer of the 1950s had to struggle to maintain 1,500 characters per second.

In 1951 MIT used CRTs on the output of the Whirlwind I computer. The technique was simple. The computer could put spots on the face of the CRT at any point on a matrix of 1024 by 1024 positions. This was good enough to plot equations and other patterns. At the same time, the University of Illinois operated CRT output in conjunction with the ILLIAC computer and used it for problems that the operator solved by trial and error. Computer-driven CRTs were then developed at MIT as part of the SAGE system to track aircraft in air defense. The extensive man/machine interaction needed was fairly well developed in the SAGE system, but it is only now that commerce and industry have accepted this level of interaction.

In the early 1950s a CRT display was used on the ORDVAC computer at Aberdeen, the spots being used to show the status of memory locations. Soon after that small CRTS were used as status displays, but these were later replaced by indicator lights. In 1965 CRTS were restored for this purpose on the CDC 6600, and they are in common use today.

Early CRT displays driven by computers required laborious programming and extensive output from the computer to form images on the screen. Each dot position had to be addressed and intensified. Since the persistence of the dot on the screen was much less than a second, the image on the screen had to be repeated or "refreshed" at a rate of something like 40 times a second to avoid flickering. Early computers had to allow enough space in their memories to hold the information while it was being refreshed on the screen.

The formation of alphanumeric characters directly from the spots was an inefficient process. In the middle 1950s the alphanumeric display generator appeared. It used coded inputs and produced alphanumeric characters anyplace on the screen; no longer was it necessary to hold a complex of dots in the computer for each character. Then a CRT display "now memory"

Fig. 17.1. Honeywell Visual Information Computer Console. In this dual-display model, one display can be used for operator messages while the other can be used for special programming formats or program queues. (*Courtesy of Honeywell Inc.*)

was added in a control unit for the CRT device so as not to use up the computer's memory. In these displays the computer needed to send information to the CRT only once for a new or updated display image. Today's displays are very much like these first alphanumeric (A/N) displays. (See Figure 17.1.)

The first large commercial sales of these displays was to the brokerage industry for stock quotation. Bunker-Ramo was a leader in the field, and IBM's 2260 came later, in 1966; it is installed in a cluster of units connected to a controller, where the refresh memory for all units resides. In 1968 came the stand-alone CRT display, which includes the CRT electronics and refresh memory in one unit, connected directly or remotely to a computer.

Graphic displays are similar to A/N displays except that they are much larger and can thus display many more numeric characters and also extensive line drawings. The graphic display is complex and is almost always used with a computer, usually a minicomputer dedicated to its operation.

Another type of graphic display, the direct-view storage tube (DVST), competes in some applications with A/N displays. It is much cheaper but does not offer extensive interaction between the operator and the computer.

A/N displays are widely used in communications systems. In remote batch and demand processing systems the display devices are connected to a local computer that is remotely connected to the main computer. The local computer can do such chores as editing, reformatting, error detection, and concentration, taking this load off the main computer. Sometimes local files can be queried and updated without interrupting the main computer. In off-line systems the displays are connected to a local storage system such as a magnetic tape cassette.

Often, CRT displays have a cursor that marks the location where the next character is to appear or the location of an existing character that is to be altered via edit controls.

The alphanumeric display is nudging out the typewriter and teletypewriter. It is fast, noiseless, flexible, and attractive. It can be entered via a keyboard or light pen as well as via the computer so that the operator can talk back to it. Airline and hotel reservation systems—wherever information must be had and updated promptly—are natural uses for it.

Microphotography

Although microfilm was seldom used commercially before 1920, it is almost as old as photography. In 1839, shortly after the introduction of the daguerreotype process, John Benjamin Dancer made the first microphotograph of a document. Dancer was England's first commerical photographer and skilled with the microscope. He put a microscope lens in his camera and produced a microsized daguerreotype.

In 1859 René Prudent Patrice Dagron got the first patent in microphotography, for viewers small enough to wear on a watch chain. His novelty jewelry enjoyed some vogue. He is better remembered for the French pigeon post, which delivered 115,000 microfilmed messages to Paris during the 1870–1871 siege.

Paris was hemmed in by the German armies, and its only contact with the outside world was via balloon or homing pigeon. Pigeons were obviously harder to shoot down. Dagron left Paris by balloon for Bordeaux and started to microfilm documents for pigeon transport. Photographs at that time were made on glass plates by the collodion process, but fortunately the developed emulsion layer could be taken from the glass and packaged into a compact roll of pigeon capacity. When the bird was debriefed, the layers of printed emulsion were unwound and spread onto a supporting medium before delivery.

After the war interest in microphotography fell off. Later on there were some important inventions (photographic film, for one), some interesting proposals (one in 1887 for recording manuscripts on microfilm), and some patents (a camera and reader in 1887, a camera to microfilm checks in 1899). The big boost to microphotography came in 1928, when G. L. McCarthy invented a flow camera for microfilming bank checks. It was so successful that other applications were found for it.

In World War II new equipment was developed and used on documents and V-mail for servicemen. Microforms other than the traditional roll (aperture cards, film jackets, micro-cards, microfiche) were produced.

Computer Output Microfilming

In the meantime the computer was developing apace, and it was discovered that microphotography could be married to the computer to get around the output bottleneck.

Graphic output was a worse problem than alphanumeric output. Some attempts were made to interface analog plotters to computers, and soon afterward the automatic digital plotter was introduced, but both gave dismal results in speed.

Altogether, the only effective output device was the cath-ode-ray tube (CRT). But although the CRT responds instantan-eously to the signals applied, the information vanishes forever once its display screen is erased. It has to be photographed. This was done by a Polaroid camera in the 1950s, and marked the dawn of computer output microfilming, or COM.

A true COM microfilmer required two further steps: a camera to record on microfilm or microfiche, and the devel-opment of coordinated processes to convert the coded infor-mation generated by the computer into the various signals required at the CRT, and to precisely register the display image on the film and automatically advance either the film or the camera to the next frame.

In 1970 the Memorex 1603 microfilm printer introduced a new imaging technique. The light-emitting ability of certain semiconductors, called light-emitting diodes, or LED, is utilized to form characters by illuminating specified diodes in an array in the familiar dot matrix. Each line of characters so formed is recorded on film, which is then advanced, instead of waiting for the completion of the entire frame, as in CRT imaging.

Thus, COM offers the user the advantage over printing of graphic as well as alphanumeric recording. It also offers

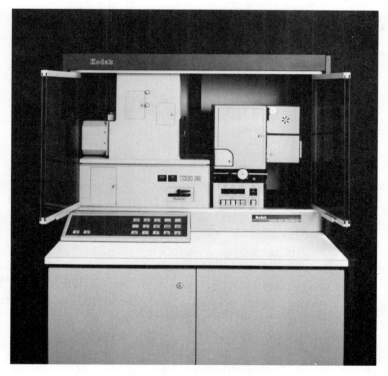

Fig. 17.2. (*Courtesy of Eastman Kodak Company*)

significant savings in cost: for example, the packing density of data imprinted on microformat is about a million and a half bits per linear inch for reduction ratios in the order of 20×. The most critical disadvantage of microfilm systems is the human problem. People don't like to use a reader instead of hard copy when a printer is not available, and don't like learning new techniques in reading and searching film.

Microfiche, a sheet of film containing a number of micro-images, uses reduction ratios from about 18× to 42×. The new ultrafiche uses ratios of 100× or more. Since a tiny scratch damages the small image, the NCR ultrafiche is placed in a laminated sandwich that protects the film but precludes its use for duplication.

All COM recorders can operate on-line with a computer and process data as it is produced, or operate off-line from a magnetic tape transport. Interface electronics are simpler for on-line operation, and the substantial cost of a tape transport is also eliminated. On-line records match or exceed many computer output speeds. However, errors cannot be detected and corrected until the film has been processed.

In addition to photographing a CRT image or an LED array, a third technique is now offered in the 3M Company electron-beam recording (EBR) procedure, which uses the electron beam of the CRT to expose a special type of film.

The Kodak KOM-90 Microfilmer is a good example of the COM devices on the market today. (Figure 17.2.)

A number of companies, including IBM and Eastman Kodak, are presently developing systems for recording digitally on microfilm. In fact, IBM has already delivered a trillion-bit storage system, utilizing the principle of spot recording, to the Atomic Energy Commission. This method simply darkens a tiny spot of film, 14 by 16 microns in size, or leaves a clear spot. These minute dimensions permit the recording of 2½ million data bits per square inch. The spots are inscribed by an electron beam that sweeps across the film. It oscillates back and forth to darken an area and cuts off if the area is to remain clear. A transparency followed by a spot is a 0, and a spot followed by a transparency is a 1.

Two experimental techniques, diffraction-grating recording and holographic recording, both depend on splitting a laser beam into two parts and reuniting them after one half has traveled a greater distance than the other. As both penetrate the emulsified layer of the film, there are places where the polarization phases reinforce and other places where the phases cancel. In the first technique the dark bands formed on the film surface after processing resemble a diffraction grating. In the second technique a two-dimensional array of black and clear squares is formed.

chapter 18

Optical Character Recognition

Computer output microfilming is one solution to the problem of getting data out of a computer. Perhaps the most promising solution to getting data into the computer is the optical character reader, which can digest information at a fast rate and, more importantly, convert printed text or numeric data directly to a form suitable for computer processing, without immediate conversion to a coded medium.

Optical character readers are not new. The first one was introduced in 1954 by Intelligent Machine Research Corporation (later part of Farrington Manufacturing Company). However, acceptance of these devices has been slow. They are expensive to buy and install. Early manufacturers did not have enough money for marketing and did not know how to design for the market. Users were leery of a new device that might not work. And until 1968 OCR machines could not recognize handprint, in which over 50 percent of source documents were written.

Furthermore, operation of OCR equipment cannot be slipshod. Forms, equipment, and operators must be carefully controlled by the hard work of the user.

Optical readers recognize the difference in contrast between the character and its background. Many current readers are severely limited by the type fonts they can read, and sometimes

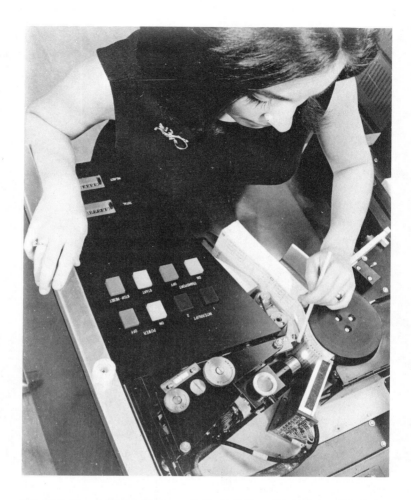

Fig. 18.1. Heart of the Honeywell Type 243 optical character document reader is the optical reading unit. The machine can
read up to 1,110 documents per minute, scanning up to 70
numerals on each document on a single pass. The OCR unit
also reads, through the small silver and black unit to the right
of the optics, documents that contain pencil marks in
preprinted areas. (*Courtesy of Honeywell Inc.*)

by the size of the characters they can handle. Some optical readers do not require special fonts and can be adjusted to read most and even all fonts, but so far this capability has proved too expensive for most users. The least expensive units are restricted to one font, usually one especially designed for low error rates and often limited to numerics plus a few special symbols. (See Figure 18.1.)

The OCR system has proved useful for credit cards, utility billing, and retail charge accounts and billing. The U. S. government is using it to process various documents, including employees' quarterly tax returns. The Post Office is the largest potential user.

Some OCR devices handle documents that have been retyped in a standard type font and format. However, the cost of retyping documents removes the cost advantage of OCR over code readers, magnetic-ink character readers, high-performance buffered keypunches, keytape, and keydisk.

A code reader recognizes the relative position of the printed input on the paper, whereas a character reader identifies the input by its shape. Mark-sense code readers are often used for grading tests. Bar-code readers, which sense thick lines or bars to represent characters, are popular with oil companies. The Datatype Company has brought out an inexpensive optical reader that reads a code imprinted by a special Selectric typewriter ball, and Potter Instrument Company has brought out a magnetic version. Magnetic-ink character readers (MICR), confined mostly to the banking industry, can handle only special type fonts printed in magnetic ink. The standard bank font is E13B. (Figure 18.2.)

True OCR readers read documents and pages of various sizes plus journal tape. The reader/punch reads data printed on 80-column tab cards and punches the data into the same cards. Microfilm optical character recognition (MOCR) devices have recently come on the market. Instead of retyping, these devices

1234 56 789 ⅠⅠ▪

Fig. 18.2. Type font E-13B.

use off-line microfilming as an intermediate step between printed paper and the scanner.

Some OCR systems must interface with a computer for encoding; others operate off-line and have an integral controller and output device. Remote OCR (ROCR) terminals transmit characters (usually by facsimile) to a remote recorder for recognition.

In OCR, as in tape and other devices, a big headache is feeding the paper or other input into the device. The transport often costs more than the device proper. Hand-fed OCR readers are cheaper but slower. In addition to the transport, an OCR reader has a scanner and a recognition unit.

The transport feeds in the documents or roll of paper at one end and disposes of it via an output stacker or other unit at the other end. The scanner, like the human eye, converts the optical images on a document into some analog or digital representation that can be analyzed by the recognition unit—the brain of the device. It compares patterns from the scanner against stored reference patterns and either identifies the patterns or rejects them as unidentifiable. Since the recognition unit is usually a large computer or a small special-purpose computer, this unit has benefited from developments in computer technology in the way of lower prices, faster memories, and better software.

The common types of scanners are mechanical disks, flying spots, parallel photocells, and vidicon scanners. These units scan mechanically, by the movement of the document or the mirrors of an optical lens system, or electronically, by the movement of sensors over the document.

The mechanical disk scanner uses a lens system and a

rotating disk with slits to focus reflected light samples onto a photosensitive device, which converts the light samples into signal pulses one character at a time.

In a flying-spot scanner a beam of light is generated in a CRT and deflected in a scan pattern. A lens system projects this light spot onto the document, from which it is reflected into a phototube. Here it generates a voltage signal proportional to the amount of reflected light. These signals are fed directly to the recognition unit in analog form or first transformed into digital form.

The use of a vertical column of photocells speeds up scanning by simultaneously sampling a number of points which, when combined, add up to a complete vertical slice of the character. The electric signals generated by the photocells are then quantized into black, white, or gray levels, and this data is fed into shift registers and stored until the entire character has been scanned. One variation of this sampling method eliminates shift registers by using a full "retina" or matrix of photocells to scan an entire character instead of just a slice. This method increases reading speed to about 2,400 characters per second. This is the fastest method so far devised, but it is expensive because as many as 800 photocells may be needed for alphanumeric character sets.

A totally different type of scanner projects characters onto a vidicon TV camera tube and scans the active surface with an electron beam. The resulting video signals are quantized to give digital values of black and white.

There are several common types of recognition units. Matrix matching stores the signals in a digital register connected to a series of resistor matrices, each representing a single reference character. A voltage output from a second digital register is compared with the voltage that would be output from the reference character.

Stroke analysis differentiates characters by the number and

position of vertical and horizontal strokes. A special-purpose computer matches the formation of the unknown character against a character truth table for the reference character.

Curve tracing is a new concept. It can accommodate fairly wide variations in shape and size of characters and thus handle handwriting. It traces the curves of the character and identifies it by certain features such as character splits and the juncture, direction, straightness, and magnitude of lines.

Analog waveform matching is based on the principle that each character passing under a read head produces a unique voltage waveform as a function of time. The waveforms of characters are matched with reference waveforms. Reading speed is some 500 characters per second. The drawback is that only a limited number of characters have unique waveforms.

Frequency analysis is used for fonts consisting of closely spaced vertical lines. The widths of the gaps between the vertical lines are measured by variations in magnetic flux. A character is identified by comparing the sequence and number of its narrow and wide gaps with stored codes for each alphanumeric character. The technique is fast and can handle a full character set.

One use for OCR is in turnaround billing, where the customer returns both the bill and his payment and the document is read into the computer again to record the payment.

People can read a document and supply missing letters or guess at a misspelled word easily enough from the great store of reference information in the human mind, but building this so-called context recognition into an OCR device is very difficult. Another OCR problem is dirt. Creases, holes, or smudges on a document in effect change the character shapes of the letters. An oil delivery man is likely to degrade an OCR record by his greasy hands. Poor printing—blurred imprints, skewed lines, and misregistered characters—also degrade input.

Fig. 18.3. Electronic retina computing reader—document carrier/ink-jet printer. (*Courtesy of Recognition Equipment Incorporated*)

The use of OCR will probably increase as devices become more realistic. Designers have tried for high speeds, but the cost of speed is out of all proportion to the advantage. New OCR devices will use integrated circuits, standard peripheral equipment, minicomputers for recognition logic and control, and manual feed in lower-cost machines. More special-purpose machines will come on the market.

chapter 19

The Future of EDP

We have seen the development of calculating machines crawl along at a snail's pace for two centuries and then accelerate into a brilliant explosion of technology that can send space ships to the moon. Will this acceleration continue? Shall we see further astonishing changes in computers?

No.

Computers are now big business; there are over 70,000 of them in use. There are hundreds of thousands of computer professionals and technicians. By the end of this decade, information processing may be the first or second largest industry in the world. The future development of an industry of this size will be governed by economics, not by the newest engineering techniques. Such techniques will not be put to use abruptly if they mean a great displacement of the existing systems in which so much money has been invested.

The freest field for new techniques is in new applications of the computer. There is much unexplored computer territory in education, health care, science, finance, and industrial control.

One of the most fertile fields is in office procedures. For years we have concentrated on improving the productivity of the farm and the factory, but there has not been a similar sharp improvement in the productivity of the office. For example, the time it takes to produce a letter has been shortened by perhaps

20 percent, partly by the electric typewriter but perhaps just as much by the correction fluids that have replaced the eraser. But labor costs for a typist have gone up more than 100 percent in the past 20 years. The solution does not lie in simply reducing to machine terms what we have always done and putting it on a computer, but in rethinking and redesigning office procedures and getting rid of many useless functions dictated by custom rather than by reason.

The office function needs an information systems design such as was used in the Apollo space flights. This kind of design has not been forthcoming because to date it would not have paid off. No company could afford the investment necessary to study the issues, design a system, train people to accept and adapt to the changes, and merchandise the product in sufficient quantity to show a profit.

The picture may change in the next two decades, partly because government regulations and other factors will make office paperwork unmanageable by current methods, and partly because the men and women who will manage our businesses will have learned to accept and use the computer as we have learned to accept and use the automobile.

Our accomplishments in the effective application of computers have not kept pace with our progress in hardware and software technology. We are supposed to have reached the fourth generation in technology, but we have hardly reached the second generation in applications. There is still a great future in computers for people with imagination.

We also need to control the abuse of the computer. Our privacy is being invaded by files kept on us by the FBI, the Defense Department, credit bureaus, marketing people. The IRS files are no longer private, but are crossbred with social security and welfare files. So many people have access to these files that information is easy to steal. The computer has also bred some very ingenious rogues who are adept at embezzlement by computer, particularly in time-sharing systems.

As we have seen, the interest of Pascal and Leibnitz in calculating machines was a derivative of their interest in philosophy. Philosophy was *the* learning, and the various sciences split off from it. In those days learned men took all knowledge to be their province.

We need to reverse the trend toward narrow specialization, particularly with respect to the computer, and to think of our new devices in relation to all the other arts and sciences. For instance, how can we use the computer creatively in medicine, politics, social science, urban planning, and a general improvement of the quality of life?

We badly need a philosophy of the computer; we need a Pascal or a Leibnitz to tell us how to fit the computer into the scheme of things for better rather than for worse.

Bibliography

Adler, Irving. *Thinking Machines: A Layman's Introduction to Logic, Boolean Algebra, and Computers.* New York: John Day Company, 1961.

Auerbach, Isaac L. Computer Technology Forecast. Speech at the IFIP Congress, August 1971, Ljubljana, Yugoslavia.

Auerbach, Isaac L. Looking Ahead—Business Data Processing Systems. Speech at the 20th Anniversary of Rome Air Development Center, June 10, 1971.

Auerbach Publishers Inc. *Standard EDP Reports.*

Babbage, Charles. *Passages from the Life of a Philosopher.* Longmans, Green, 1864.

Babbage, Charles, and others. *Selected Writings by Charles Babbage and Others.* Edited and with an Introduction by Philip Morrison and Emily Morrison. New York: Dover Publications, 1961.

Barlow, Alfred. *The History and Principle of Weaving by Hand and by Power.* London: Sampson Low, Marston, Seule, & Rivington; Philadelphia: Henry Carey Baird & Co., 1878.

Bernice, Daniel D. *Introduction to Computers and Data Processing.* Prentice-Hall, 1970.

Bernstein, Jeremy. *The Analytical Engine.* New York: Knopf/Random House, 1963.

Broome, J. H. *Pascal.* New York: Barnes and Noble, 1965.

Davis, Gordon B. *An Introduction to Electronic Computers.* New York: McGraw-Hill, 1965.

Derry, T. K., and Williams, Trevor I. *A Short History of Technology from the Earliest Times to A.D. 1900.* New York and Oxford: Oxford University Press, 1960.

Dodd, K. N. *Logical Design for Computers and Control*. Philadelphia: Auerbach Publishers Inc., 1972.

Eckert, W. J., and Jones, Rebecca. *Faster, Faster: A Simple Description of a Giant Electronic Calculator and the Problems It Solves*. New York: McGraw-Hill, 1955.

EDP Almanac. "Data Management," January 1972.

Freebury, H. A. *A History of Mathematics*. New York: Macmillan, 1961.

Funk & Wagnalls. *New Standard Encyclopedia*, 1931.

Goldstine, Herman H. *The Computer from Pascal to von Neumann*. Princeton University Press, 1972.

Halacy, Dan. *Charles Babbage, Father of the Computer*. New York, Macmillan, 1970.

"Introduction to System/360." Publication R-29-0256-1. Endicott, New York: IBM, 1968.

Menninger, Karl. *Number Words and Number Symbols*. Cambridge: MIT Press, 1969.

Morison, Elting. *Men, Machines, and Modern Times*. Cambridge: MIT Press, 1966.

Neugebauer, O. *The Exact Sciences in Antiquity*. Princeton University Press, 1952.

New York Times, June 1947. "Harvard Unveils Huge Calculator."

New York Times Magazine, May 4, 1932. "Baron Wolfgang von Kempelen's Turk."

Ortega y Gasset, José. "The Barbarism of Specialization." In *Great Essays in Science*, Gardner, Martin (ed.). Pocket Library, 1957.

Ortega y Gasset, José. *The Idea of Principle in Leibnitz and the Evolution of Deductive Theory*. Adams, Mildred (translator). New York: Norton, 1971.

Pascal, Blaise. *Great Experiment Concerning the Equilibrium of Fluids*. 1663.

Pascal, Blaise. *Thoughts: Selections*. The Great Books Foundation, 1949.

Pullan, J. M. *The History of the Abacus*. Washington, D.C.: Praeger.

Rosenberg, Dr. Jerry M. *The Computer Prophets*. New York: Macmillan, 1969.

Serrell, R., Astrahan, M. M., Patterson, G. W., and Pyne, I. B. "The Evolution of Computing Machines and Systems." *Proceedings* of the IRE, May 1962, p. 1039-1.

Shaw, Ruth Lydia. *Leibnitz*. Penguin Books, 1954.

Turck, J. A. V. *Origin of Modern Calculating Machines*. Chicago, 1921. Published under the auspices of the Western Society of Engineers.

Turing, Alan M. "Can a Machine Think?" *The World of Mathematics*, vol. 3, Newman, James (ed.). New York: Simon & Schuster, 1956.

UNIVAC Corporation. *The Origin and Evolution of UNIVAC Computer Systems.*

Von Neumann, John. "The General and Logical Theory of Automata." *The World of Mathematics*, vol. 3, p. 2070, Newman, James (ed.). Simon & Schuster, 1956.

The Works of Geoffrey Chaucer. Poll, Alfred W., et al. (eds.). London: Macmillan, 1926.

Glossary

Abacus An early manual calculating device, consisting of counters moved around on a board, beads strung on parallel wires, or—more primitively—marks made on the ground.

Accumulator A device that stores the augend and when the addend is received, adds the two numbers and stores the sum. The actual adding is done within or by the accumulator. In some applications, the accumulator can be cleared; in others, it can control or modify another quantity in another register or location of storage. It can also serve as the register of the arithmetic and logic unit.

Algol (Algorithmic Language) A computer language for handling mathematical problems.

Alphanumeric A contraction of alphabetic-numeric, sometimes further contracted to alphameric. A set of alphanumeric characters includes letters, numerals, and usually additional special symbols for punctuation, etc.

Analog computer A computer in which variables are represented by analogous physical or electrical magnitudes, such as rotation or voltage, and the solution of the problem is shown by the varying behavior of the physical system. Most analog computers offer solutions continually in real time.

Arithmetic unit The part of the computer which contains the circuits necessary for arithmetic operations such as add, subtract, multiply, divide.

ASCII American Standard Code for Information Exchange.

Assembler language A computer language in which one instruction causes one event in the computer—that is, there is a one-to-one correspondence with the machine language of the computer.

219

Auxiliary storage   A storage that supplements the primary or central processor high-speed storage of a computer. It usually has higher capacity, lower speed, and lower cost than the primary storage.

Bar code   A code that uses bars of various dimensions.

BASIC (Beginner's All-Purpose Symbolic Instruction Code)   A computer language that resembles FORTRAN but is simpler and easier to learn.

Binary system   A number system with a base of 2 (instead of the base 10 of the decimal system).

Biquinary   A mixed-radix number system in which each decimal digit is represented by two digits, AB, where A equals 1 or 0 and B equals 0, 1, 2, 3, or 4; for example, the biquinary representation of 7 is 12.

Bistable   Able to assume either one of two stable states. In computers, a bistable device can store a bit of information, since a zero can be assigned to one state and a one to the other. A flip-flop is a bistable circuit.

Bit   A binary digit.

Boolean algebra   An algebra of classes and propositions dealing with truth values as variables. It is a branch of symbolic logic, named for George Boole (1815-1864), and can be utilized in the design of logic and switching circuits in a computer.

Buffer   A storage device used to hold computer data temporarily and sometimes to manipulate it. Data may be transformed in the buffer to the format of the receiving medium. A buffer is not a separate device, but a dedicated section of a storage device.

Byte   A small group of adjacent binary digits operated upon as a unit.

Calculus   1. A method of mathematical analysis or calculation which uses a special symbolic notation. 2. The combined mathematics of differential and integral calculus.

Carrier wave   An electromagnetic steady-state wave that can be modulated in frequency, amplitude, phase, or otherwise to transmit visual, auditory, or other information.

Carry mechanism   A device for transferring the overflow of a column in a number system to the next left, or more significant, column. The overflow arises when the sum of two or more digits exceeds the base of the number system.

Cathode-ray tube (CRT)   A vacuum tube in which an image is formed on a screen inside the face of the tube by the deflection of a beam of electrons in two dimensions.

Central processing unit The part of a computer that contains the arithmetic, logic, and control circuits necessary to interpret and execute instructions.

Channel A small computer that controls input-output devices on a computer and thus relieves the central processing unit of this work.

Clamp circuit A circuit that prevents the electrical potential of one point from exceeding a certain value with reference to another point. In computer logic circuits the clamp is designed to hold a certain part of a waveform at a certain voltage level.

COBOL (Common Business Oriented Language) A computer language for developing programs and printing reports.

Coincident-current selection In an array of magnetic cores, the selective switching of one core by applying two or more drive pulses to the array at the same time, which have a compounded effect in one core only. Each core has a magnetizing threshold below which switching will not occur.

COM *See* Computer output microfilming.

Common carrier A person or company that provides communication or transport services to the general public for a fee; e.g., AT&T, Western Union, the Penn Central Railroad, TWA.

Compiler A computer program that translates a symbolic language such as FORTRAN into machine language.

Computer Technically, a device that accepts data and makes high-speed mathematical or logical calculations or otherwise processes the data according to a predetermined program and produces the results in printed or other form.

Computer output microfilming The process of converting digitized computer output into a corresponding image of alphanumeric or graphic forms and automatically recording successive images on a sequenced microformat.

Core image library A section of the system residence storage which holds programs that can be loaded directly into main storage for execution.

Core storage A storage consisting of an array of magnetic cores (shaped as ferrite rings, toroids, metal tapes on bobbins, etc.). Each core can store one binary digit. Core storages are high in speed and random in access, and are usually activated by coincident current.

Counter A piece of wood, metal, or other material, sometimes resembling a coin, moved around on the board of an abacus to make calculations.

Counting board   A ruled board on which counters are moved to perform calculations; an abacus.

CPU   *See* Central processing unit.

CRT   *See* Cathode-ray tube.

Cryogenics   The study and utilization of phenomena that occur at extremely low temperatures. A cryogenic element is a circuit that utilizes the phenomena of superconductivity and low thermal noise at or near absolute zero, and usually the destruction of the superconductivity by magnetic fields.

Cursor   A movable indicator such as a hairline on a slide rule or an illuminated arrow on a visual display.

Cybernetics   The theoretical study of control processes in mechanical, electronic, and biological systems; e.g., the comparison of communication and control in data-handling machines and in the nervous system of animals. Initiated and named by Norbert Wiener (from Gr. *kubernetes*, a governor or steersman).

Dashpot   In its usual form a dashpot consists of a cylinder with a piston. It may be used to dampen the motion of instruments that are vibrating by attaching the piston to the instrument part and the cylinder to the frame. As the piston moves, the fluid in the cylinder—which may be air, oil, or water—squeezes past the piston and offers resistance to the motion. The resistance generated depends on the velocity of the piston in relation to the cylinder, the closeness of fit between the two, and the viscosity of the fluid. When the fit is close and the fluid is air, a partial vacuum is formed that produces a pull on the piston, and in this form the dashpot is sometimes used to serve as a spring.

Data cell storage   Wedge-shaped cells containing strips of magnetic tape, which can be wound around a drum for reading and writing.

Data communications system   A collection of functional units for transferring digital data between two or more terminals.

Data processing   The manipulation of raw information according to rules for some special purpose, such as creating an ordered file or solving a mathematical problem.

Dedicated communication line   A line in a communication network allocated for a specified use or user.

Delay line   A logic element in which the input sequence undergoes a delay of a specified time. Delay lines are used to introduce time lag into the transmission of data, usually to bring data from several points at different distances to the same place at the same time;

and to store data by recirculating it through a continuous line. Acoustic, electromagnetic, and magnetic delay lines are based on the respective time of propagation of these waves. Magnetostrictive and piezoelectric phenomena are used to launch and sense sonic pulses in acoustic lines.

Demodulation The elimination of a carrier wave and the recovery of the original modulating wave.

Differential analyzer A computer, usually analog, that solves differential equations. It may be mechanical and use interconnected mechanisms such as gears, cams, and disks; or it may be electronic and use interconnected electronic integrators.

Diffraction grating A polished metal surface, usually of glass or metal, with a large number of very fine parallel grooves or slits cut in the surface. It is used to produce optical spectra by the diffraction of light.

Digital Pertaining to data in the form of digits; in discrete form.

Digital computer A computer that performs operations on quantities represented as digits.

Diode An electronic device such as a tube or transistor with two terminals, which permits current to flow through it in only one direction. It can serve as a rectifier or detector. The diode, in particular the crystal diode, is used in the logic elements of computers.

Discrete Constituting a separate, distinct thing; or consisting of separate, distinct parts.

Drag In flying, the retarding force exerted on the airplane by the air.

Drawloom A loom on which patterns can be woven in cloth by varying the number and position of the warp threads to be raised.

EBCDIC Extended Binary Coded Decimal Interchange Code.

EBR *See* Electron beam recording.

Electromechanical device A device that is partly electric and partly mechanical in its components and operation; e.g., an electric egg beater.

Electron tube A sealed tube with a high vacuum or controlled quantity of gas so that electrons can move freely enough to act as the principal carriers of current between at least one pair of electrodes.

Electron beam recording A technique in computer output microfilming which uses the electron beam of a CRT to expose a special type of film.

Electronic   Pertaining to or utilizing the motion, emission, and behavior of currents of free electrons and certain ions, especially in vacuum tubes, gas tubes, semiconductors, and superconductors. Any distinction between electronic and electrical is usually made on the basis of the kind of current-carrying medium or device.

Electrostatic storage   A storage device that stores data in the form of electrically charged spots or regions on a nonconducting surface such as the screen of a CRT. A binary digit is represented by the presence or absence of such a spot. The data needs to be regenerated or "refreshed" continually and restored after it is read since it is destroyed by reading. One form of reading is to direct a stream of electrons at the spot; an external pulse is caused if there is no charge.

Fail-safe device   A device that can automatically compensate for a failure.

Fiber optics   The study of the transmission of light by internal reflection through flexible, extremely fine glass fibers.

Field   A number of consecutive columns on a punched card reserved for specific kinds of information.

Flip-flop   A circuit or device capable of assuming either one of two stable states, the state being changed by an input stimulus. A flip-flop can store one bit of information and is used in the counters and registers of digital computers to store numbers and to hold gates open or closed. In this application the flip-flop is usually a two-tube or two-transistor device in which only one tube or transistor is conducting at a time.

Floating-point arithmetic   A system for manipulating the decimal point in a number in order to represent it by fewer digits; e.g., a decimal number is represented by a decimal fraction times a power of 10.

FORTRAN (Formula Translation)   A computer language for handling scientific and engineering problems.

Gate   A circuit, widely used in computers, that has an output dependent on some function of its input.

Griff   An arrangement of parallel bars in the Jacquard loom which lifts the hooked wires that raise the warp threads.

Hardware   The physical equipment of a data processing system as distinct from data, programs, or routines.

Heddle   In weaving, a device through which warp yarn is threaded, the raising or lowering of which creates a shed.

Hexadecimal system   A numerical system with a base of 16.

Higher-level language A computer language in which one instruction normally causes more than one machine instruction to operate.

Holography The production of images by the reconstruction of wavefronts; it is generally done by using lasers to record photographically a diffraction pattern from which a three-dimensional image can be projected.

Hybrid computer A computing system containing both analog and digital elements.

Initial program loader A manually loaded program that starts the automatic operation of the supervisor program.

Instruction A statement that defines an operation to be performed and gives the values or locations of all operands.

Integrated circuit An electronic circuit in which the active and passive elements are all formed from a single piece of semiconducting material by controlling the purity and geometry of the conducting paths. It is usually a complete unit and cannot be disassembled. Some such circuits are formed by etching on a germanium crystal; in others transistors and diodes are inserted in a thin ceramic wafer and resistive and conductive inks are deposited to form resistors, etc.

Interrupt A signal marking or requesting a change in the operation of a computer.

Inverter (or Negation element) A device which can reverse a signal, condition, state, or event into its opposite. In a computer it is a logical device which changes a binary input to its opposite value.

I/O Input-output.

Jetton (Fr. jeton) A piece or counter moved on a counting board to perform calculations. (From Fr. *jeter*, to throw or cast.)

Job control program A program which controls the basic independent unit of work done by the operating system of a computer.

Jovial (Jules' Own Version of the International Algebraic Language) A computer language similar to Algol used for mathematical problems.

Keydisk (or key-to-disk) device A device for entering data directly on disks by a keyboard.

Keytape (or key-to-tape) device A device for entering data directly on tape by a keyboard.

Laser (light amplification by stimulated emission of radiation) A device that converts incident light waves of mixed frequencies to one or more highly amplified and coherent discrete frequencies. The term is also sometimes applied to devices such as the maser, which operate in the same way in invisible regions of the electromagnetic spectrum.

LED *See* Light-emitting diodes.

Librarian A computer program that maintains, services, and organizes the libraries of the operating system in a computer.

Light-emitting diodes Diodes made from semiconductors which have the ability to emit light. They are used to form characters by illuminating specified diodes in an array or dot matrix.

Light pen A photosensitive device that is held against the face of a CRT, where its position can be determined by a computer. Thus points or lines can be drawn on the tube and successive coordinates can be put into the computer storage. A computer program can compare these coordinates with reference figures and cause the display of the true figure (e.g., a circle) instead of the approximation drawn by the pen, and can manipulate the figure in size, rotation, etc. The light pen enables the operator to interact with the computer.

Logarithm The exponent showing the power to which a fixed number, the base, must be raised to produce a given number; e.g., if $a^x = b$, the logarithm of b, with a as the base, is x.

Logic The study of the principles of reasoning or argument. Symbolic logic analyzes formal logic by means of a formal artificial language, such as a symbolic calculus or Boolean algebra, to avoid the inconsistencies and ambiguities of ordinary language. A logic element in a computer is a device which performs a function that can usually be represented by logic operators in a symbolic representation; e.g., AND, OR.

Logical unit The part of the computer that contains the circuits necessary for logical operations such as comparing, moving, shifting, and editing.

Machine language The actual set of symbols that the computer hardware can interpret; it is usually written in binary.

Magnetic disk storage Storage of data on flat circular plates with a magnetic surface by the selective magnetization of spots as the disk rotates. The recording tracks are concentric circles. The recording heads can usually be moved radially and positioned precisely. Disk storage devices that have a number of reading and recording heads offer some degree of random access. A disk storage unit, consisting of a number of disks, offers better volumetric storage density than the magnetic drum.

Magnetic drum storage A storage device consisting of a rotating cylinder coated with a magnetic material. Data is stored in the form of magnetized spots read and written in circular rings by magnetic read-write heads. Locations are addressable by the position of the heads and the angular position of the drum.

Magnetic ink character recognition (MICR) A method of processing documents, widely used in banks. Standard characters are pre-printed with magnetic ink on such documents so that they can be identified and sorted by a magnetic sensing device.

Magnetic tape storage Storage of computer data on a tape usually made of metal or plastic coated with a magnetic material. The tapes are usually several mils thick and 0.25 to 2 inches wide, and have 5 to 10 tracks, packing up to several thousand binary digits per inch along each track, and linear speeds equivalent to up to 100,000 bits per second in each track. In many tape devices a character of 5 to 8 bits is placed across the tape, and groups of these characters form words serially along the tape. The tapes are wound on reels, and advanced continuously or intermittently for reading and writing data when a section of the tape passes under a magnetic head.

Magnetostrictive effect The deformation, or development of propor-tional mechanical strains, in ferromagnetic material when it is exposed to a magnetic field.

Main storage Storage or memory that is an integral part of the primary computing system; sometimes called internal or primary storage.

Mark sensing The sensing of a mark made with an electrographic pencil with a conductive lead. The marks are made according to a position code. This system is often used for grading examinations.

Memory *See* Storage.

MICR *See* Magnetic ink character recognition.

Microfiche A rectangular sheet of film containing microimages re-corded in rows and columns and photographed at reduction ratios from $18\times$ to $42\times$.

Microfilm A film on which documents are photographed in reduced sizes for storage and viewing, and possibly later enlargement and printing.

Microminiature   Extremely small; microminiature components or circuits are those that have been reduced in size below the so-called miniature size. Miniature parts are usually small parts packed tightly. Microminiature circuits are usually constructed as integrated units by etching and deposition techniques.

Microphotograph   A photograph made in reduced size so that it may need to be enlarged for viewing.

Microwave   A superhigh-frequency radio-band electromagnetic wave, in the range from 1,000 to 300,000 megahertz.

Minicomputer   A small computer. A typical minicomputer might cost $25,000, have a memory of 4K, a central processor, and one input-output device such as a teletypewriter; software would consist only of assembly language and FORTRAN.

Mnemonic   Intended to assist human memory. A mnemonic computer language is one in which the symbols resemble English words (or words in the language of the programmer).

Modem (Modulator/demodulator)   In a communications terminal the modulator and demodulator circuits are normally mounted together on one panel and may have common elements. The unit is called a modem.

Modulation   The variation of some characteristic of a wave (frequency, amplitude, phase) by the action of another wave; e.g., the variation in frequency of a carrier radio wave in accordance with the audio frequency of a modulator wave. One form of modulation is keying, or turning a carrier wave on and off, as in Morse code.

Monad   According to the philosophy of Leibnitz, an impenetrable and indivisible unit which is the basic building block of the physical world.

Monolithic integrated circuit   A unit in which several electronic circuits, such as gates and flip-flops, are etched on a single crystal or other semiconductor material. They are made by etching and deposition processes.

Multiplexer channel   A small computer, which may transmit information from an input device or to an output device one byte at a time, thus interleaving messages from or to more than one device.

Multiprocessing   Simultaneous processing and input-output operations in a computer.

Object program   A program written in machine language. It is usually formed by translation from a program written in a symbolic language.

OCR   *See* Optical character recognition.

Octal system   A numerical system with a base of 8.

Off-line equipment   Equipment not in direct communication with or under the control of the principal equipment in a system; e.g., a keypunch that operates independently of the main system in preparing input.

On-line equipment   Equipment in direct communication with, or under the control of, the principal equipment in a system; e.g., a printer that is connected to, and controlled by, the central processing unit of a computer.

Operating system   A file of programs required for the operation of a computer.

Optical character recognition (OCR)   The machine reading of printed characters by the use of light-sensitive materials or devices.

Oscillography   The projection of a pattern of electric signals on the face of a CRT.

Oscilloscope   An instrument with a CRT which gives a visual representation of changes in a varying current or voltage.

Parallel processing   The simultaneous processing of two or more items, which may be parts of a whole. "Parallel by bit" refers to the handling of all the binary digits of a byte or character at the same time in separate equipment such as wires, switches, or gates. Parallel by character refers to the similar handling of all the characters of a computer word.

Parity bit   A bit added to a group of bits, such as a character or word, to make the number of 1s or 0s odd or even. Whenever the character or word is operated upon in any way, a count is made to see whether the number of 1s or 0s is as specified. If it is not, an error is assumed.

Pentode   A five-electrode vacuum tube, with a cathode, control grid, screen grid, suppressor grid, and plate. If two or more of the electrodes can control the flow of current, the tube can be used as a logic element, or gate. Depending on the way in which the electrodes control the flow of current, the tube can serve as an AND, OR, NOR, or NAND gate.

Peripheral device   A part of a computer system extraneous to the basic unit of the computer, which comprises the central processor, main storage, console, and associated power supply. Peripheral devices include magnetic tape units, card readers and punches, printers, sorters, typewriters, and plotters.

Photocell (Also called **photoelectric cell, electric eye**) An electronic device whose output varies in accordance with incident radiation, in particular visible light.

Photosensitive Sensitive to light.

Phototube An electron tube with a light-sensitive cathode.

Piezoelectric effect The generation of mechanical strains in dielectric crystals placed in an electrical field, the strain being proportionate to the strength of the field; and conversely, the generation of electricity in such crystals subjected to mechanical stress.

PL/1 (Programming Language 1) A computer language that incorporates features of both COBOL and FORTRAN and can be used for both commercial and scientific work.

Place value The value given to a digit in a numbering system because of its location. Thus in the number 11 in the decimal system, the left-hand digit has a value of 10 and the right-hand digit a value of 1.

Problem or application program A computer program that directs the computer through the steps necessary to perform a specific task, such as calculating a payroll.

Program A procedure for solving a problem, coded for a computer.

Program status word A word that shows the logical status of a computer with respect to the program being run; e.g., the state of the program in the CPU and the address of the next instruction to be executed.

Quantize To divide the range of values of a variable into a number of separate intervals of definite value; e.g., to divide a length into inches or centimeters, or a temperature range into degrees.

Raster The scan pattern on a TV tube, consisting of a certain density of horizontal lines per inch.

Real time The actual time during which a physical process or event occurs. Computation done in real time is completed by the time the physical phenomenon involved is completed; e.g., the computations for a controlled-approach aircraft landing.

Refresh To re-record an image on a CRT screen when it begins to fade.

Register A device in a computer for storing a specific quantity of data, such as a word or a numeral, for some specific purpose. Registers often consist of a series of high-speed flip-flops that control logic gates, but they may consist of a row of magnetic cores or other forms of storage. A shift register can move data in the register (usually right or left) in response to signals received.

Relay   An automatic electromechanical or electromagnetic device that in reponse to a small change in current or voltage activates switches or other devices.

Ring counter   A closed loop of interconnected bistable elements, e.g., flip-flops, of which only one is in a specified state (on or off) at any one time. In counting, the element next in sequence assumes the specified state, all others being in the opposite state.

RPG (Report Program Generator)   A computer language for developing programs and printing reports.

SAGE (Semi-Automatic Ground Environment)   A real-time communications-based digital computer control system for air defense. It accepts radar data over phone lines; processes and displays it; correlates the data with known flight plans and other data; and automatically guides interception weapons.

Selector channel   A channel that transmits an entire data record from an input device or to an output device in one operation.

Semiconductor   Any of various solid crystalline substances, such as silicon or germanium, that have an electrical conductivity better than that of an insulator, such as glass or rubber, but worse than that of a conductor, such as pure metal.

Serial-parallel processing   Processing data items in both serial and parallel, such as parallel by bit and serial by character; or converting parallel data to serial data for handling over one line, such as a transmission line or serial adder. A serial-parallel converter converts serial data coming in on one wire to parallel data going out on several wires.

Serial processing   The sequencing in time of two or more processes or events; e.g., the time-sequencing of the individual parts of a whole, such as the bits of a word or the data in a message, successively on the same facilities.

Shed   The space created by raising one group of warp threads in weaving and lowering the remaining threads; the weft is inserted through this space.

Shift register   *See* Register.

Simscript   A computer language somewhat like FORTRAN, designed for programming simulations.

Simulation   The representation of the behavior of one system by another system; e.g., representing the behavior of one computer by a computer program written for, and run on, another computer; or representing the behavior of a physical system, such as an industrial process or a rocket flight, by a computer and a program. Computer simulation permits the variation of parameters to show the effect of such variation without having to alter the physical system.

Slide rule   A calculating device consisting of two or more logarithmically scaled rules arranged to slide along one another to show the mechanical equivalent of addition or subtraction.

SNOBOL   A computer language for processing lists. Other languages for this purpose are LISP, SLIP, COMIT, IPL-V.

Software   Written or printed data, such as programs, routines, symbolic languages, manuals, circuit diagrams, and operational procedures, that is necessary for the operation of a computer.

Solid-state device   Active or passive circuit elements or assemblies that utilize the electric, magnetic, or optical properties of materials in the solid state rather than in the gaseous or liquid state.

Soroban   A Japanese bead abacus widely used for business calculations.

Source program   A computer program written in a symbolic computer language such as COBOL. It must be translated into an object program written in machine language before the computer can run it.

Storage   The part of a computer that receives, holds, and subsequently releases data. Storage may be in the form of a plugboard, an array of magnetic cores, magnetic tapes or disks, an electrostatic storage tube, a delay line, a bank of flip-flops. New types of storage, such as microfilm and laser recording, are coming into use.

Supervisor   A program that supervises the selection and scheduling of problem programs and input-output functions. It is part of the operating system of a computer.

Synchronous   A mode of computer operation in which each event, such as an instruction, is controlled by a clock signal that enables the logic gates for the execution of each logic step.

System loader   A program that loads job control programs into a computer.

System residence device   An auxiliary storage unit that holds the programs of the operating system.

Tabulator   A machine that reads data from one medium, such as punched cards or tape, magnetic tape, or computer storage, and produces lists, tables, and totals on another medium such as paper sheets or forms.

Terminal In a communication network, a point at which data can enter or leave the network.

Thin-film storage A miniature system of magnetic cores, formed, for instance, by small deposits on plastic, glass, or ceramic plates connected by very thin wires. In another type the thin film is plated on wire and the intersection of a plated and insulated wire is used to produce a bit.

Time sharing 1. The use of a single device for two or more purposes; e.g., to make a device available for two different applications, one at a time, or to execute two or more programs on a computer by interleaving them. 2. The simultaneous use of a computational facility by more than one person, each remote from the facility.

Transistor A three-terminal solid-state device made of semiconductor material doped as *n*- or *p*-type. It performs most of the functions of a vacuum tube, including amplification, detection, switching, gating, modulation, demodulation.

Transport A mechanism for moving a physical recording medium into or out of a processing device; e.g., paper or magnetic tape, or documents for an optical character reader.

Triode An electronic device such as a tube or transistor with three electrodes. It is used principally as an amplifier.

Ultrafiche Microfiche holding images reduced $100\times$ or more.

Ultrasonic Above the human audio range—that is, above 20 kilohertz.

Vidicon tube A small TV camera tube that forms an image by means of charge density on a photoconductive surface, which is subsequently scanned by an electron beam.

Virtual memory or storage The use of auxiliary memory units as if they were part of the main processor storage, accomplished by fast transfer of data between the main memory and the auxiliary unit.

Warp The lengthwise threads in woven cloth.

Index